RIGHT HERE, RIGHT NOW

✝ ✝

DEVOTIONS FOR MEN

JOSHUA COOLEY

RIGHT HERE, RIGHT NOW

DEVOTIONS FOR MEN

180 READINGS FOR BUSY DAYS

BARBOUR
PUBLISHING

Cover design © Greg Jackson, Thinkpen Design

Published by Barbour Publishing, Inc., 1810 Barbour Drive, Uhrichsville, Ohio 44683, www.barbourbooks.com

Our mission is to inspire the world with the life-changing message of the Bible.

Printed in China.

Yes, life is busy— but that should be no barrier to time spent with God.

These devotions are perfect for men on the go, offering brief, thought-provoking entries that can be read

+ on an airplane

+ in a restaurant

+ hiking the trail

+ between classes

+ lying in bed

+ awaiting an appointment. . .

+ right here, right now!

In 180 entries written by and for men, *Right Here, Right Now Devotions* will inspire you to keep God in your thoughts amid the activity and stress of daily life.

Featuring scriptures from the fresh-yet-familiar Barbour Simplified KJV, these devotions will challenge you to a greater knowledge of God—and commitment to Him.

CREATOR OF ALL

In the beginning God created the heaven and the earth.

GENESIS 1:1

✦

The first verse in the Bible is wonderfully simple and strikingly powerful. And it's there for a reason. From the get-go, God wanted His original readers, the ancient Israelites, to push aside the prevailing polytheism of their day and understand that there is only one true God who created all things.

Today, pagan polytheism might be mostly relegated to the pages of antiquity. But the truth of Genesis 1:1 is every bit as powerful. The fact that there's a sovereign, eternal Creator who made and rules over the universe changes everything. If we were created, that means we owe allegiance to someone greater than ourselves. It means we would do well to seek Him, grow in our understanding and love of Him, and find out what He expects from us. It means our life has purpose. It means we are greatly loved.

God created everything we see and don't see. God created *you*. Seek Him today.

What can I do, right here, right now, to honor God as my great Creator?

AN INSPIRED WORK

No prophecy of scripture is of any private
interpretation. For the prophecy did not come in
old time by the will of man, but holy men of God
spoke as they were moved by the Holy Spirit.

2 PETER 1:20–21

✝

We often talk about inspired performances. Beethoven was surely inspired when he composed his Fifth Symphony. The same can be said for Michelangelo painting the Sistine Chapel ceiling. And Kobe Bryant must have felt a surge of inspiration when he dropped eighty-one points against the Toronto Raptors on January 22, 2006.

No inspired work, though, is like the Word of God.

In scripture, we have the literal words of God to us. From Genesis to Revelation, God spoke His truth to us through human authors "as they were moved by the Holy Spirit." Likewise, 2 Timothy 3:16 assures us that "all scripture is given by inspiration of God."

Every time we open God's Word, we are reading the very words of the Creator and Ruler of the universe.

What can I do, right here, right now,
to better know God's Word?

A SURE HOPE

*Now faith is the substance of things hoped
for, the evidence of things not seen.*

HEBREWS 11:1

We hope our upcoming job performance review goes well.
We hope our retirement account trends upward. We hope
our loved one beats cancer.

We hope for all these things—and much more—in life.
But we don't know for sure. The outcome isn't guaranteed.
We use the word *hope* in these contexts, but it's as much
wishful thinking as anything.

When it comes to our faith, the Bible paints a completely different picture. Our faith in Christ isn't wishful
thinking, hesitant expectation, or guarded optimism. Faith
is a sure hope—a rock-solid belief—in something that isn't
seen but is guaranteed to be true. Our faith is firm trust in
the claims of holy scripture—that God created the world,
redeems lost sinners through Christ, and will bring His
children into His presence forever one day.

We don't see these things with our eyes now, but we
believe them with our hearts. That's biblical faith. That's
a sure hope.

**What can I do, right here, right now,
to show faith—sure hope—in Christ?**

WHAT IS PRAYER?

Truly God has heard me; He has attended to the voice of my prayer. Blessed is God, who has not turned away my prayer or His mercy from me.

PSALM 66:19–20

Prayer, like breathing, is one of the most vital aspects of the Christian life. Yet it's something we as believers often fail to do. Perhaps we don't fully understand what prayer is.

Prayer is simply talking to our heavenly Father. It's a beautiful gift and privilege, not a rote or liturgical exercise. It's an act of worship that expresses trust and reliance on someone besides ourselves for everything in our lives. And He listens and answers!

Abraham prayed. Moses prayed. David prayed. Hezekiah prayed. Daniel prayed. Nehemiah prayed. Paul prayed. Even Jesus prayed—and often. We should too.

When we pray, we approach the holy throne of the Lord God Almighty, maker of all things. We are accessing the power, grace, and love of heaven.

Why wouldn't we pray?

What can I do, right here, right now, to make prayer a daily part of my life?

ORIGIN STORY

"He gives to all life and breath and all things, and has made from one blood all nations of men to dwell on all the face of the earth...that they should seek the Lord."

ACTS 17:25–27

✛

Nice try, Chuck!

Yep, Charles Darwin sure did give it a go with *The Origin of Species* and his theory of evolution. It's quite a convenient explanation to support a humanistic worldview.

After all, if Darwin is correct and all life on earth really did originate from cosmic chance, we, as humans, are the ultimate source of truth, knowledge, and morality. We make the rules! We control our own fate! Let's party!

But ol' Charles was off. Way off. There is, in fact, an all-knowing, all-powerful Creator. And as such, He makes the rules, not us. We are eternally beholden to Him.

The reality of divine creation changes everything. We answer to God and must seek after Him. Any other pursuit in life is sheer monkey business.

What can I do, right here, right now, to orient my life to God's purposes?

NO SPARE CHANGE

*The counsel of the LORD stands forever,
the thoughts of His heart to all generations.*
PSALM 33:11

✦

Change is a constant part of our lives.

We change clothes every day (hopefully). We change a baby's diapers. We change lanes while driving. We change hairstyles, addresses, phones, cars, churches, classes, schools, jobs, and careers. We change our minds. We change our plans. Sometimes it feels like we do nothing *but* change.

Thankfully, God and His sovereign purposes never change. He is always perfectly good, and His plans never shift. He will always accomplish His will—in our lives and in the world at large.

When you think about your purpose in life— understanding and pursuing God's will—remember that the counsel of the Lord stands forever. What He has decreed will always come to pass. What He has designed in ages past will come to fruition, guaranteed. This should give us great hope—and some peace amid the constant change.

**What can I do, right here, right now, to rest
in the good, unchanging purposes of God?**

GROUND ZERO OF GOD'S REDEMPTIVE PLAN

The house of God. . .is the church of the living
God, the pillar and ground of the truth.

1 TIMOTHY 3:15

✠

When God redeemed His old covenant people from Egyptian slavery through Moses, He created the nation of Israel and gave them the law. But when God redeemed His new covenant people (we as Christians today) from slavery to sin through Jesus, He created the church, "the pillar and ground of the truth," and gave us the full gospel of Christ.

The church is now ground zero for God's redemptive plan. It's headquarters. The staging area. The launching pad.

This is incredible. God could have chosen any number of ways to miraculously redeem the lost and create for Himself an eternal family. In His sovereign wisdom, He chose to do this by creating the church—transforming sinners through Christ into a worldwide group of believers from every nation and language who worship Him.

If you're a believer, praise God that you are part of His great church.

**What can I do, right here, right now,
to be faithful in God's church?**

PLACED JOY

You have put gladness in my heart.

PSALM 4:7

As humans, we are on a relentless quest for joy. There's no end to what we'll try to fill this need: money, fame, pleasure, relationships, work, travel, adventure, leisure, electronics, technology, drugs, alcohol—you name it. Not all these things are bad, and some can be helpful. But none of them will bring complete fulfillment to us.

True joy only comes from God.

As David wrote in Psalm 4:7, God is the one who puts gladness in our hearts. True joy. Lasting joy. Purposeful, meaningful joy.

And don't miss this truth: Ultimately, any true joy we discover doesn't come to us through our own search or tireless efforts. God *places* it in our hearts. He sent His Son to be the sacrifice for our sin. Then He opens our spiritually dead hearts to repent, accept the truth of the gospel, and receive the joy of new life in Christ.

**What can I do, right here, right now,
to receive the joy God offers in Jesus?**

EXPECTED HARDSHIP

*Beloved, do not think it strange concerning
the fiery trial that is to test you as though
some strange thing happened to you.*

1 PETER 4:12

When Peter wrote his first epistle to first-century Christians in ancient Asia Minor, they were being persecuted for their faith. The date was likely the early AD 60s, during the rule of Roman Emperor Nero, whose animosity toward Christians is well-documented.

These persecutions were not trivial. Twice, Peter described them with the metaphor of fire (1 Peter 1:7; 4:12). Christians were misunderstood, mocked, and alienated. They were falsely accused, dragged to court, and stripped of possessions. They were beaten, imprisoned, and put to death.

Peter made it clear that Christians should expect trials. They don't take God by surprise. They don't force Him to enact Plan B. They are within His good, sovereign providence.

When you face trials not of your own making, "rejoice because you are partakers of Christ's sufferings" (4:13). Christ's glory will soon be your own (4:14).

**What can I do, right here, right now,
to not be surprised by life's trials?**

THREE IN ONE

The grace of the Lord Jesus Christ and the love of God
and the communion of the Holy Spirit be with you all.
2 CORINTHIANS 13:14

✚

One of the core doctrines of Christianity is God's triune nature. He is one God existing in three persons—Father, Son (Jesus), and Holy Spirit.

All persons are equal in nature but distinct in their roles. The Father created the world, rules over it, and sent His Son to save us from our sins. The Son fulfilled the Father's plan of salvation through His atoning death and miraculous resurrection. And the Spirit applies the salvation that the Son provided, convicting us of sin, regenerating spiritually dead hearts, and sanctifying believers.

We call God's three-in-one nature the "Trinity," even though that word is never explicitly mentioned in the Bible. Still, scripture is filled with references to God's triune nature, including Matthew 3:16–17, Acts 7:55, and 1 John 4:2.

The doctrine of the Trinity is as mysterious as it is marvelous. But it's critical to believe.

**What can I do, right here, right now,
to grow in my understanding of the Trinity?**

PERFECT IN EVERY WAY

The law of the Lord is perfect, converting the soul.
The testimony of the Lord is sure, making wise the simple.

PSALM 19:7

Brooks Robinson is widely regarded as the greatest defensive third baseman in Major League Baseball history. In a 23-year career, the Baltimore Orioles' Hall of Famer won sixteen Gold Gloves—more than any other infielder ever—and had a .971 fielding percentage, almost exclusively at the hot corner.

Of course, that fielding percentage isn't flawless. As great as he was flashing the leather, "Brooksy" still made 263 errors. Nobody's perfect...nobody, that is, except God.

And so is His Word. We can trust the entirety of the Bible because it comes from God Himself. He doesn't make mistakes, so His words are without error. Jesus confirmed this in His high priestly prayer: "Your word is truth" (John 17:17).

In a volatile world, isn't it good to know that scripture is a bedrock of truth? God's Word has always been perfectly true and without error, and it always will be.

What can I do, right here, right now, to grow in my gratefulness for God's perfect Word?

PLEASING GOD

*Without faith it is impossible to please Him, for he
who comes to God must believe that He is, and that
He is a rewarder of those who diligently seek Him.*

HEBREWS 11:6

Throughout history, humans have concocted every con-
ceivable idea to try to please God.

We have tried to follow the Old Testament law flaw-
lessly. We have performed elaborate sacrifices, rituals, and
ceremonies. We have given Him everything—even down
to our mints, herbs, and spices. We have washed our gar-
ments, shaved our beards, and put on our Sunday best. We
have gone into solitude in the mountains and constructed
majestic cathedrals in the cities. We have gone to church for
Tuesday morning Bible studies, Wednesday night prayer,
and two services on Sundays. We have perfected piety.

Yet none of this impresses God. He wants us to
acknowledge Him as Lord over all, admit our utter depravity, and repent of our sins. He wants us to trust in His Son
for salvation and believe all His promises.

God wants our faith.

What can I do, right here,
right now, to rest in faith?

TALKING TO THE GOD
WHO ALREADY KNOWS

"When you pray, do not use vain repetitions as the heathen do. For they think that they shall be heard for their many words. Therefore do not be like them. For your Father knows what things you have need of before you ask Him."
MATTHEW 6:7–8

Jesus gave us the Lord's Prayer, the great template of talking to God, while rebuking the hypocritical religious leaders of first-century Israel. He wanted His followers to pray as a means of worshipping God, not trying to impress anyone.

We can't move God with pious words. God knows all things, including every thought we have before we speak (Psalm 139:4). When we pray, we're not telling God anything He doesn't already know. Prayer is a humble acknowledgement of His comprehensive rule in every aspect of our lives.

Rather than trying to inform or impress God in prayer, we should simply kneel before Him, confessing His great providence, compassion, and wisdom. He will move in prayer, not because of our loquaciousness, but because of His overwhelming grace and love.

What can I do, right here, right now, to approach the throne of grace in humility?

A MATTER OF LIFE AND DEATH

"I have set before you life and death, blessing and cursing.
Therefore choose life, that both you and your descendants
may live, that you may love the LORD your God and
that you may obey His voice and that you may cling to
Him, for He is your life and the length of your days."

DEUTERONOMY 30:19–20

The wilderness wanderings were over.

After forty years of experiencing God's judgment for rebellion and unbelief, Israel was perched on the doorstep of Canaan, ready to enter the Promised Land. There, on the plains of Moab, Moses gave the people a choice: life or death, blessing or cursing. If the people obeyed God, they would receive life and enjoy countless blessings. If they rejected Him, they would be under His curse and suffer death.

That decision is still before us today. Faith and obedience to God will bring us life. But rejection of God, His commands, and His plan of salvation through Christ will bring utter ruin.

The choice is clear!

What can I do, right here, right now,
to choose life and blessings from God?

PURSUING HIS OWN GLORY

"Blessing and honor and glory and power be to Him who sits on the throne and to the Lamb forever and ever."
REVELATION 5:13

If someone you know—say your boss, pastor, spouse, or even a casual acquaintance—told you one day, "My ultimate purpose is my own glory," you'd probably raise a concerned eyebrow. Yet this is exactly what God says about Himself. Above all, God pursues His own glory.

Perhaps you're thinking, *Well, that sounds a bit self-serving.* And it certainly would be if anyone other than God pursued that. But God is not like us. He is not small, sinful, selfish, finite, and limited in knowledge. He is awesome, holy, righteous, infinite, and all-knowing. His ways are far above ours. His glory always results in our good.

When God is exalted, His people rejoice. When God is glorified, we are blessed! So, like David in Psalm 86:12, we proclaim, "I will praise You, O Lord my God, with all my heart, and I will glorify Your name forevermore."

**What can I do, right here,
right now, to rejoice in God's glory?**

THE POWER OF COMMUNITY

*They continued steadfastly in the apostles' doctrine and
fellowship and in the breaking of bread and in prayers.*

Acts 2:42

From the first moments of creation, God knew human isolation wasn't ideal. Shortly after God created Adam, He said, "It is not good that the man should be alone" (Genesis 2:18), so He gave Adam a companion.

Our lives work best in community. That's why Jesus began His church shortly after His death, resurrection, and ascension. The apostles' gospel-fueled journeys throughout the Roman Empire were never to create a group of disassociated individual believers, but to birth a worldwide network of believers linked by a common faith. First-century Christians began gathering weekly in house churches to hear the preaching of God's Word, pray, and fellowship (Acts 2:42).

Two thousand years later, it's just as important for us to gather regularly. We weren't meant to do this alone. We need the spiritual strength and mutual encouragement that comes from uniting together in Christ until He returns. God's church is a gift to us.

**What can I do, right here, right now,
to embrace Christian community more?**

JOYFUL ARRIVAL

When they saw the star, they rejoiced
with exceedingly great joy.
MATTHEW 2:10

Of all the news we could ever hear in life, is there anything better than knowing our sins will be paid for, peace between us and a holy God will be restored, and eternal life will be freely given to all who believe?

This is the joyful, incomparable reality that Jesus brought with His first advent. When the wise men heard about it, "they rejoiced with exceedingly great joy." When Elizabeth, Mary's relative, heard about it, baby John "leaped for joy" in her womb (Luke 1:44). When the angels appeared to the shepherds near Bethlehem, they brought "good tidings of great joy" (Luke 2:10). After beholding the infant Savior, the shepherds told others the joyful news, "glorifying and praising God" (Luke 2:20).

The coming of Christ—and all He would accomplish— is like nothing else the world has ever seen. In our busy, often difficult, lives, let's pause to reflect on this exceedingly great joy.

What can I do, right here, right now, to rejoice
in what Christ has done on my behalf?

CASTING CARE

*Humble yourselves under the mighty hand of God,
. . .casting all your care on Him, for He cares for you.*

1 PETER 5:6–7

✛

One of the hardest—and most common—aspects of trials is the tendency to think God doesn't care about what we're going through.

Some of the great saints of old cried out, "How long, O Lord?" Even the angel of the Lord did so (Zechariah 1:12)! And when Jesus slept as a storm threatened to sink the boat He was on, the disciples pleaded, "Master, do You not care that we are perishing?" (Mark 4:38).

Of course God cares—more than we can fathom. Trials don't indicate His neglect, absence, or abandonment. Trials are part of His amazing—and often inscrutable—plan. Incredibly, in God's economy, trials actually *show* He cares. They draw the faithful toward Him and make us more like our Savior.

So when life's storms howl and you feel like you're sinking, humble yourself before God and cast your cares on Him through prayer and faith.

He cares for you.

**What can I do, right here,
right now, to cast my cares on God?**

SOVEREIGN POWER

*"I know that You can do everything and that
no thought can be withheld from You."*

JOB 42:2

Men love tools. Especially power tools!

Well before Tim "the Tool Man" Taylor entertained us with his fictitious foibles on the 1990s TV show *Home Improvement*, tools were a fixture in men's garages, sheds, kitchen cabinets, and—going back a bit further—caves and mud huts. We love the power and abilities that tools provide. But as actor Tim Allen (not to mention our own experience) humorously reminded us, there's a limit to our power and abilities.

Not so with God.

One of the great truths of scripture is God's sovereignty—His ability to do anything according to His perfect will. In a world rife with the limitations and evils of human power, isn't it good to know there's a holy God in heaven who has all power and sovereignly rules over everything, from the orbits of planets to the minute details of our daily existence? Praise the Lord!

**What can I do, right here, right now, to rest
in God's sovereign control of my life?**

PROPER AUTHORITY

Righteous You are, O LORD, and upright are
Your judgments. Your testimonies that You have
commanded are righteous and very faithful.
PSALM 119:137–138

Authority seems like a taboo concept in society today. Because human authority figures at all levels are finite and fallible, it's easy to distrust anything that sets itself up as someone, or something, with power and influence in our lives.

But the Bible is different. Scripture holds authority in all areas of our lives because of its Author.

God is not human. He is not fallible, and neither is His Word. The authority of scripture flows from the authority of God, who is righteous, faithful, and true. Because God is the Creator and Ruler of the universe and He is the essence of truth, we can trust the authority of His divinely inspired Word.

In a world filled with human authority that consistently fails, that is a comforting thought indeed.

**What can I do, right here, right now,
to submit to scripture's authority?**

THE NATURE OF
SAVING FAITH

For by grace you are saved through faith,
and that not of yourselves; it is the gift of God,
not of works, lest any man should boast.

EPHESIANS 2:8–9

We know we cannot please God without faith (Hebrews 11:6–8) and salvation comes through faith, not good works (Galatians 2:16). But how do we get the faith necessary to experience God's salvation? If we muster up this saving faith within ourselves, wouldn't that very faith become a "good work" to merit our own salvation?

Paul answers this in Ephesians 2:8–9. He confirms salvation comes "by grace...through faith." But notice: This is "not of yourselves; it is the gift of God, not of works, lest any man should boast." Our salvation is 100 percent "by grace"—including the very faith that saves us.

Spiritually dead human hearts (Ephesians 2:1; Colossians 2:13) cannot magically self-generate a saving faith. In God's amazing love, His Spirit regenerates dead hearts (Ezekiel 36:26) and produces the faith we need for redemption. All of salvation—even our faith—is a gracious gift of God!

What can I do, right here, right now,
to grow in my understanding of saving faith?

HALLOWING THE NAME

"Pray according to this manner: Our Father
who is in heaven, hallowed be Your name."
MATTHEW 6:9

For centuries, Christians have been reciting the Lord's Prayer—Jesus' great example of how to pray in Matthew 6:9–13. This is beautiful and good. But above all, Jesus meant for the Lord's Prayer to be a model for speaking with God. And it's no accident that He started the Lord's Prayer the way He did.

When we pray, we should approach God with worshipful hearts, acknowledging who He is ("Our Father who is in heaven") and praising Him ("hallowed be Your name"). To "hallow" is to revere and worship. It's to lift high, honor, and venerate. It's to give credit where credit is due.

Before we approach the throne of grace with all our cares, worries, and desires, it's good to acknowledge *whom* we approach. This will color the rest of our prayer. This will help us leave pride and presumption at the door of heaven's throne room and enter instead with humility. Our Father in heaven is worthy of it.

What can I do, right here, right now,
to enter my prayers with praise?

HEART SURGERY

"I will also give you a new heart, and I will put a new spirit within you. And I will take away the stony heart out of your flesh, and I will give you a heart of flesh."

EZEKIEL 36:26

As Moses told the Israelites before they entered the Promised Land, the decision whether or not to follow God is really a matter of life and death (see page 20). But the Bible also makes it clear that we are lost in sin and incapable of following Him on our own (Romans 3:10–18, 23). So what are we to do? Is the situation hopeless?

Not at all.

Following God begins when we realize that the faith and obedience He requires is all a work of His grace. As Ezekiel 36:26 says, God must first perform a spiritual heart transplant on us, giving us the capacity to obey. He does this by a work of His Spirit, opening our hearts to receive the truth of the gospel. Then, by His Spirit, we can walk in His ways (Ezekiel 36:27).

What can I do, right here, right now, to joyfully receive "a heart of flesh"?

THE HIDDEN AND REVEALED WILL OF GOD

"If the Lord wills, we shall live and do this or that."
JAMES 4:15

✚

What is God's will for me?

At some point, every Christian has applied this question to a variety of decisions in life, such as:

Does God want me to marry this person?

Does God want me to take this job?

Is this truly the house I should buy?

Then we often get frustrated when we don't hear a clear voice from heaven proclaim, "Yes, John, marry Gertrude."

We need a better understanding of God's will.

As Deuteronomy 29:29 says, God's will contains both secret and revealed elements. God's secret will was decided in eternity past. It will come to pass, but He has chosen not to show us certain things. God's revealed will—which is expansive and sufficient—is found in His Word. Obey God's revealed will, and trust His hidden one. All the while, humbly pray and plan in the posture of James 4:15—"If the Lord wills"—as you seek His direction.

What can I do, right here, right now, to follow God's revealed will in scripture and trust Him for the rest?

FED BY THE WORD

Let the word of Christ dwell in you richly in
all wisdom, teaching and admonishing one
another in psalms and hymns and spiritual songs,
singing with grace in your hearts to the Lord.

COLOSSIANS 3:16

In the nascent days of the Christian church, between the day of Pentecost (Acts 2) and the New Testament writings, the first Christians met together regularly—in large part to listen to the apostles' teachings.

At that point, there were no written records of Jesus' world-changing life, death, and resurrection. So the early Christians sat under the teaching of Spirit-inspired eyewitnesses who had experienced all Jesus did and taught.

Today, we have the benefit of full, authoritative scripture in two testaments. But we still need to be fed with truth from God's Word. Personal time in scripture is critical to our spiritual health, but so is gathered fellowship in a gospel-centered, Bible-centric church.

Like our spiritual ancestors, we must continue "steadfastly in the apostles' doctrine" (Acts 2:42) by teachers who faithfully give "witness of the resurrection of the Lord Jesus" (Acts 4:33).

**What can I do, right here, right now,
to commit to a Bible-teaching church?**

JOYFUL NOURISHMENT

*"These things I have spoken to you, that My joy might
remain in you, and that your joy might be full."*

JOHN 15:11

✚

The Gospel of John records Jesus' famous seven "I am"
statements. These are metaphors Jesus used to teach something important about Himself while also pointing to His
divinity, hearkening back to God's great self-revelation to
Moses: "I Am That I Am" (Exodus 3:14).

Jesus' final "I am" statement came during the Last
Supper when He told His disciples, "I am the true vine"
(John 15:1). Jesus' followers, He said, are the branches, and
"He who abides in Me, and I in him, the same brings forth
much fruit. For without Me you can do nothing" (verse 5).

Just like a grape withers when disconnected from the
grapevine and a tree branch dies apart from the trunk, we
will never find real purpose apart from Jesus.

He renews our hearts. He feeds our souls. He gives us
life. True joy is found in following Christ. Remain in Him.

**What can I do, right here, right now,
to remain in Christ, the true vine?**

A PERFECT ENDING

*Let patience have its perfect work, that you may
be perfect and complete, lacking nothing.*

JAMES 1:4

Have you ever worked backward in math to solve a problem? Sometimes it helps to start with the final answer, then go in reverse to better understand the path toward the solution. Similarly, as we seek to understand the trials of life, let's look at the ultimate goal, then go backward.

The ultimate goal is God's glory, which is achieved in large part by our glorification—the moment Jesus returns, renews all things, and completes our sanctification in His eternal presence. At that moment, we will lack nothing.

God could certainly snap His omnipotent fingers and instantly bring all this about. But what would that achieve? How would our appreciation for His faithfulness and goodness be stoked? Where would faith come from? How would we grow?

So God uses many things, including trials, to get His children to the ultimate goal. Be patient. He is doing a perfect work in you with a glorious culmination.

**What can I do, right here, right now, to be patient
through life's hardships with the end goal in sight?**

KNOWLEDGE IS POWER

Great is our Lord and of great power;
His understanding is infinite.

PSALM 147:5

People once thought the earth was flat. Astronomers once assumed the sun and planets revolved around the earth. To replenish tired athletes, coaches used to withhold water and give them salt tablets instead. *Beavis and Butt-Head* used to be a popular TV show.

Clearly, there's a limit to human knowledge and understanding. God, on the other hand, is omniscient. He possesses perfect knowledge and wisdom.

This is a staggering—and wonderful—truth. What a joy to know that the God we serve knows everything! But God's knowledge is not only informational; it is also intimate. Yes, He knows every single digit after the decimal in π, but He also knows the number of hairs on your head (Matthew 10:30). He knows your thoughts, fears, and dreams. He knows every word you'll say before you speak it (Psalm 139:4). He knows your past, present, and future. He knows all the good plans He has for you (Jeremiah 29:11).

Aren't these comforting thoughts?

What can I do, right here, right now, to know
more about the God who knows me perfectly?

LIVING AND POWERFUL

For the word of God is living and powerful and sharper
than any two-edged sword, piercing even to the dividing
of soul and spirit, and of the joints and marrow, and is
a discerner of the thoughts and intentions of the heart.

HEBREWS 4:12

Many people appreciate the Bible as a historical document that sheds light on ancient cultures. They might even admit it has modern value as a volume of moral principles. However, they stop short of calling it the inspired, inerrant, authoritative Word of God that is relevant to all aspects of our modern lives.

But that's exactly what scripture is. The Bible is not an ancient relic or dusty artifact. It's the "living and powerful" Word of God! It spoke God's perfect truth for life and salvation to its original readers, and it does the same for us today.

Cultures change and time passes, but our need for redemption is just as great today as ever. Scripture shows us the way.

What can I do, right here, right now, to make scripture a living and active part of my life?

THE GREAT SWAP

*To him who does not work, but believes in Him who
justifies the ungodly, his faith is counted for righteousness.*
ROMANS 4:5

Let's say you own a baseball card shop and a guy walks
in with a mint-condition 1951 Bowman Mickey Mantle
rookie—one of the most coveted cards in the business. He
suggests a straight-up swap: his Mantle rookie for a 1989
Topps Dave Otto that's collecting dust in your "commons"
bin. Would you make that trade?

Oh yeah! You'd be getting a small fortune for pennies.

When we put our faith in Christ, we get the deal of
a lifetime. Romans 4:5 says our "faith is counted for righteousness." In other words, God credits us with Jesus' perfect
obedience. What are we offering in return? Nothing but
our sin and shame. Nothing of spiritual value whatsoever.

Yet Jesus went to the cross so that divine, life-changing
swap could be made. Through faith, our sins are imputed to
Him, and His righteousness is imputed to us (2 Corinthians
5:21). Thank you, Jesus!

**What can I do, right here, right now,
to savor the imputation of Christ?**

ADVANCING THE KINGDOM

*"Your kingdom come. Your will be done
on earth as it is in heaven."*

MATTHEW 6:10

We are quite adept at building our own little kingdoms on earth. Our lives our consumed with our families, jobs, relationships, church, money, bills, and cleaning the gutters. Nothing bad in and of itself, but our prayers can quickly become myopically focused on the immediate here and now.

But life isn't about building our kingdoms. Life is about advancing the kingdom of God. And our prayers should reflect this.

Do your prayers indicate that you're most concerned with your own personal fiefdom? Or do the prayerful desires of your heart gravitate toward what God wants to do on earth through His children until the Lord Jesus returns?

One day, God will wipe away all earthly strivings, renew His creation, and set up an eternal kingdom of peace and righteousness. Why not start praying for the advancement of that glorious kingdom now?

**What can I do, right here, right now, to focus
my prayers on building God's kingdom?**

SAYING VS. DOING

"If you love Me, keep My commandments."
JOHN 14:15

✚

If you have kids—or have been around them—you know that a kid saying something and doing something can be two completely different things.

"Billy, go clean your room."

"Okay, Mom, I will in just a minute."

Ticktock, ticktock. . .

It's the same in our spiritual lives. There are many who claim to be Christians—a term that means "follower of Christ." But there are far fewer who actually do what Christ commands. As Jesus said in Matthew 7:21, "Not everyone who says to Me, 'Lord, Lord,' shall enter into the kingdom of heaven, but he who does the will of My Father who is in heaven."

Works don't save us—Jesus does—but keeping Jesus' commandments is a natural outpouring of love and obedience toward the Savior who gave His life for us.

Those who truly follow the Lord obey Him in word and deed. Those who truly love Jesus keep His commandments.

**What can I do, right here, right now,
to put my words into action?**

THE ONE WHO IS GREATER

*"My thoughts are not your thoughts, nor are your
ways My ways," says the LORD. "For as the heavens
are higher than the earth, so are My ways higher than
your ways and My thoughts than your thoughts."*

ISAIAH 55:8–9

As we seek to understand God's will and our purpose in
life, it would greatly benefit us to let Isaiah 55:8–9 sink
deep into our souls.

God spoke those words to the rebellious nation of
Judah through the prophet Isaiah. The people had rejected
God and tried to find their own path. God was calling
them to humble themselves and acknowledge His rule.

God's ways and His will are far different—and infinitely
greater—than our own. We would be wise, then, to align
our ways and wills with His. But how?

We start by acknowledging that God is far greater
than us and that His ways are far better than ours. Then,
as we submit to Him, we "shall go out with joy and be led
forth with peace" (Isaiah 55:12).

**What can I do, right here, right now,
to acknowledge God's sovereignty in my life?**

HEAD OF THE CHURCH

*He has put all things under His feet and gave Him
to be the head over all things to the church, which is
His body, the fullness of Him who fills all in all.*

Ephesians 1:22–23

Christ is the head of the church.

Christians immediately assent to this. But do we fully grasp the meaning?

Ephesians 1:22–23, which describes Jesus' lordship over the church, finishes a long, rich train of thought from the apostle Paul, who laid out God's entire plan of salvation from eternity past in the preceding twenty-one verses. After the Son fulfilled the Father's timeless redemptive plan, the Father placed the Son as head of His worldwide family of believers.

This is glorious—yet it doesn't always feel so, what with our denominational factions, infighting, spiritual apathy, cult-of-personality pastors, and church hurt. But those problems are on us, not God.

Jesus sits enthroned in heaven as head of His church while also actively walking among it (Revelation 2:1). We would do well to pause and reflect on this.

**What can I do, right here,
right now, to regard the church as fully
under the lordship of Christ?**

40

THE JOY SET BEFORE HIM

Looking to Jesus, the author and finisher of our
faith, who for the joy that was set before Him
endured the cross, despising the shame, and is
seated at the right hand of the throne of God.

HEBREWS 12:2

The passion of Jesus—His arrest, trials, torture, and crucifixion—was the greatest miscarriage of justice and one of the most horrific forms of execution in human history. We should continually thank Jesus for how He suffered on our behalf to reconcile sinners like us to a holy God.

Yet Hebrews 12:2 points out a truly astounding facet of Jesus' passion: "the joy. . .set before Him." As Jesus suffered unimaginable pain—none more so than bearing the full wrath of God and the temporary loss of perfect fellowship with the Father (Matthew 27:46)—He nevertheless had joy in mind. What was this surprising joy in the midst of terrible suffering? To become "the author and finisher of our faith."

Today, rejoice that Jesus endured such agony for the joy of your salvation.

**What can I do, right here, right now,
to praise Jesus for enduring the cross for me?**

A DIFFICULT GUARANTEE

All who will live godly in Christ
Jesus shall suffer persecution.
2 TIMOTHY 3:12

✚

As Benjamin Franklin wisely noted, few things are certain in life except death and taxes. Maybe a few other things too, such as gravity, inflation, rush-hour traffic, and crooked politicians. Christians can add persecution to the list.

While trials are a natural part of life for everyone in a fallen world, followers of Jesus should expect a unique variety of trials—those related to their faith. Jesus stated it bluntly to His disciples: "You shall be hated by all men for My name's sake" (Matthew 10:22). Paul affirmed this in 2 Timothy 3:12. The world has always been hostile to Jesus and His followers—and always will be until His return.

What should our response be? Faithfulness and perseverance. "Continue in the things that you have learned and have been assured of," Paul wrote (2 Timothy 3:14). And we have this assurance from the Lord Jesus Himself: "He who endures to the end shall be saved" (Matthew 10:22).

What can I do, right here, right now, to prepare for the time I'm persecuted for my faith?

FAIR PLAY

"I am the LORD who exercises loving-kindness,
justice, and righteousness on the earth.
For in these things I delight," says the LORD.

JEREMIAH 9:24

✚

That's not fair!

This is a phrase every parent knows quite well. From an early age, children have an innate sense of justice. When they catch even the smallest whiff of perceived injustice—say, their little brother getting three scoops of ice cream to their two—they sound the alarm for all to hear.

Are we adults much different? We rail against the injustices in society, politics, our workplaces, our neighborhoods, and, yes, even our marriages. We want justice, fairness, and rightness.

Aren't you glad that God is always just, fair, and right? We don't serve a fickle god who delights in zapping us when we misstep. We serve a God who delights in righteousness and truth. All His ways are perfect. This means we can always trust Him—in every situation in life.

What can I do, right here, right now,
to be fair and just to others in my life?

INVALUABLE ASSET

The law of Your mouth is better to me
than thousands of gold and silver.

PSALM 119:72

✚

When the Queen of Sheba visited King Solomon, she brought him a lavish gift of one hundred twenty talents of gold, among other valuables. The gold alone was worth hundreds of millions of dollars in today's currency.

But that was a drop in the financial bucket for ol' Solly. His annual gold imports totaled 666 talents (1 Kings 10:14). Yet Solomon's glittering vaults—indeed, all the world's material wealth—pales in comparison to the value of God's Word.

Earthly riches will fade. But God's words are eternal. As Jesus said in Matthew 24:35, "Heaven and earth shall pass away, but My words shall not pass away."

A stack of Benjamins certainly doesn't hold the words of eternal life. Neither do precious metals, rare jewels, or access to Elon Musk's checkbook. But the Bible does. Only there do we find everything we need for this life and the life to come. So treasure God's Word!

What can I do, right here,
right now, to treasure God's Word?

PEACE WITH GOD

*Therefore, being justified by faith, we have peace
with God through our Lord Jesus Christ.*

ROMANS 5:1

Peace.

We all want it in our lives, but it can feel so elusive. Our fallen world is filled with wars and rumors of wars. There's conflict in politics, schools, and sports. On a personal level, we often experience upheaval and strife in our jobs, churches, families, and marriages. Worst of all, we all start out life at war with God (Ephesians 2:1–3), lost in our sin and rebellion.

But there's good news. As Romans 5:1 affirms, faith in Christ brings justification and peace with God. Through Jesus, the sovereign ruler of the universe no longer holds our sin against us. Our debt is satisfied. The ransom payment for freedom from sin and death is fully paid.

Conflict will still linger in our lives until Jesus returns. But reconciliation with a holy God is our greatest need in life, and it's available through faith in Christ.

**What can I do, right here, right now,
to experience spiritual peace in life?**

DAILY NEEDS, OPEN HANDS

"Give us this day our daily bread."
MATTHEW 6:11

✤

We eat bread daily. And fruit. And vegetables. And meat. And dairy products. And dessert. And seconds on dessert. And. . .well, hopefully not thirds.

Most of us don't live hand to mouth. We are abundantly blessed, and we often take our daily needs for granted. But they are a gift from God, not a given.

In the Lord's Prayer, Jesus teaches us to rely on God for all our daily needs, including the ones that seem to come so readily. As James 1:17 says, "Every good gift and every perfect gift is from above and comes down from the Father of lights."

We are a weak and needy people. Ultimately, everything we have is from the Lord—even our daily bread. Praying for our daily needs acknowledges this. It's a posture of humility to the God who gives, takes away, and loves showering His children with good gifts.

What can I do, right here, right now, to rely on God for my daily needs?

TRAINING FOR GLORY

I discipline my body and bring it into subjection,
lest that by any means, when I have preached
to others, I myself should be disqualified.

1 CORINTHIANS 9:27

When Paul penned his great athletic metaphor in 1 Corinthians 9:24–27, he had in mind the biennial Isthmian Games in Corinth—a sporting event similar to our Olympics. Then and now, the principle holds true: Just like an athlete training to win a prize, our spiritual success cannot be achieved without discipline and focus.

True Christianity isn't merely "fire insurance" or a Sunday social club. It's an abiding faith that manifests itself in obedience and humble service. We must fight the "old self" and put on the new. It requires dedication, focus, and discipline. It takes hard work and commitment to a single-minded purpose: eternal glory.

Like a world-class athlete who dedicates himself solely to one cause, let's embrace the self-denial and discipline that comes with following Christ.

What can I do, right here,
right now, to train my body—heart,
mind, and soul—to honor the Lord?

GLORIOUS CONCEALMENT

It is the glory of God to conceal a thing.
PROVERBS 25:2

✠

If you are a parent, you know the feeling—and frustration—of a child trying to hide something from you. It can be sad to see a child pursuing deceitfulness—and a little annoying that your child thinks so lowly of your observation skills. When there's a crumb trail from the empty cookie jar to your child's bedroom, it doesn't take Sherlock Holmes' powers of deduction to figure out what happened.

But it's different with God. When God conceals a matter, it's not because He is embarrassed or trying to hide wrongdoing. Far from it! Proverbs 25:2 says it's His "glory" to conceal certain things. Some other translations use terms such as *honor* and *privilege*.

Would a God whose will could be fully known by sinful mortals be great? Would a God whose ways were completely obvious to limited beings such as ourselves be praiseworthy?

Hardly.

Praise God that He has the glory, honor, and privilege to both reveal and conceal.

**What can I do, right here, right now,
to enlarge my view of God?**

WEEKLY ENCOURAGEMENT

*Let us consider one another to provoke
to love and to good works.*

HEBREWS 10:24

Quick! Get the kids in the car!

Fly down the road, honking at those who dare obey the speed limit.

Drop the kids off in children's ministry and hustle to find a good pew seat, hopefully avoiding the woman who tries to sing "Great Is Thy Faithfulness" as a soprano...but shouldn't.

Listen to announcements, say "amen" a few times during the sermon, and hustle home for the rest of the day. Because, after all—football!

Too often, this is how we treat church. Yet the writer of Hebrews, in the context of lauding corporate worship, tells us to consider how to "provoke" each other "to love and to good works."

At church, do you pursue deeper-than-surface-level conversations with fellow believers? Do you actively encourage others? Do you serve regularly in a ministry?

Let's approach church as it's meant to be: a place to use our gifts to edify the body of Christ.

**What can I do, right here, right now,
to provoke others to love and good works?**

JOY IN BELIEVING

*Now may the God of hope fill you with all joy
and peace in believing, that you may abound in
hope through the power of the Holy Spirit.*

ROMANS 15:13

✚

God can do whatever He pleases according to His perfect
will. He has ordained everything in human history, and
nothing happens outside His providential care.

He doesn't need us, but amazingly, He chooses to work
out His plans in and through us.

When we are harassed by hardships or struggling with
faith, God could choose to instantly infuse us with all the
joy and peace we need. But in His sovereign wisdom and
love, He chooses a better way. Romans 15:13 says He gives
us joy and peace "in [our] believing." It's often incremental,
according to our faith.

True spiritual joy doesn't just happen. As we trust in
God's character and promises, His Spirit fills us with the
joy, peace, and hope we need.

Are you lacking today? Believe in the Lord and His
goodness, and He will give you what you need.

**What can I do, right here,
right now, to seek joy in God?**

BLESSED PERSECUTION

*"Blessed are those who are persecuted for righteousness'
sake, for theirs is the kingdom of heaven."*

MATTHEW 5:10

From scripture and our own experiences, it's clear that
human existence is rife with trials. God's Word also affirms
that many of these trials will involve persecution for our
faith in Christ.

But Jesus revealed an additional and remarkable truth
about this in the Beatitudes: When people revile us for
following Jesus, we'll be *blessed* for it.

This sounds oxymoronic at first. But it's not. Spiritually
speaking, the world doesn't revile its own. Blend in and no
one will notice. But if you build your life on Christ and
proclaim His name, you'll be different. The world will notice,
and it will react. Just as Jesus felt rejection, you will too.

On that day, no matter how hard it is, you'll be in good
company. "Rejoice and be exceedingly glad," Jesus said, "for
great is your reward in heaven, for so they persecuted the
prophets who were before you" (Matthew 5:12).

**What can I do, right here,
right now, to suffer well for Christ?**

UNCHANGING

*"For I am the LORD; I do not change.
Therefore you sons of Jacob are not consumed."*
MALACHI 3:6

The average NASCAR pit stop takes twelve seconds or less. In the amount of time it takes a kid to say his ABCs, a professional pit crew can change four tires and fill a gas tank.

That's good change. (And honestly, it makes you wonder why the local auto shop needs all morning to replace your tires!)

But not all change is good. Aren't you glad that God *doesn't* change? Imagine if He did. If God could change for the better, that means that the version of God we first trusted in wasn't perfectly holy, wise, powerful, and good—like He claims to be in scripture. And if God could change for the worse, well, that's a terrifying thought indeed.

But God never changes. We as believers aren't consumed by the whims or emotions of a fickle deity. No! Instead, we are enveloped in God's unchanging love, grace, forgiveness, and eternal purposes for His children. Thank You, Lord!

**What can I do, right here, right now,
to become more spiritually consistent?**

NIGHT LIGHT

Your word is a lamp to my feet and a light to my path.

PSALM 119:105

Thank goodness for Thomas Edison.

Okay, okay. So Edison didn't actually invent the light bulb. But he gets much of the credit for the incandescent bulb, which propelled society forward in countless ways.

Can you imagine life without light bulbs? Or life before the light bulb's predecessor, gas-powered lighting? Can you imagine living in utter darkness—save for torches, oil lanterns, and the pale light of the moon—after sunset? This is the context in which the psalmist wrote Psalm 119:105.

Just like the ancients needed lamps and torches to light shadowy paths at night, we need God's Word to light our way in a world darkened by sin. Struggling with faith? Turn to the Bible. Need godly wisdom? Open scripture. Feeling stressed or discouraged? Rest in the Word.

In all aspects of life, let God's Word light your way.

**What can I do, right here, right now,
to follow the light of scripture?**

WORK IT OUT

For as the body without the spirit is dead,
so faith without works is also dead.
JAMES 2:26

✚

Sola fide.

This Latin phrase was one of the five core *solas* of the great Protestant Reformation of the sixteenth and seventeenth centuries. It means "faith alone." In fighting against the fallacious doctrines of the Roman Catholic Church at that time, Martin Luther and other Reformers insisted that we are justified by God's grace alone, through faith alone, not by works.

But the apostle James writes in James 2:26 that "faith without works is. . .dead." Is there a conflict here?

No—James is declaring a vital truth. Works play no part in our salvation, but they do reveal the genuineness of our faith. Faith that doesn't produce good works and ongoing sanctification in Christ was never really true faith at all.

Christ fulfilled all the spiritual merits we'll ever need. We do good works, therefore, out of hearts that are obedient to God, grateful for His grace, and excited to build His kingdom.

What can I do, right here, right now, to share my faith with others through good works?

FORGIVENESS, GIVEN AND RECEIVED

"Forgive us our debts, as we forgive our debtors."
MATTHEW 6:12

In Matthew 18, Jesus shared one of His most piercing parables. In the story, a great king mercifully forgave one of his servants an unpayable debt. Then the man went out and mistreated one of his fellow servants for owing him a relative pittance. The king condemned the wicked servant for his hypocrisy and threw him in debtor's jail until the king was repaid.

This parable should influence our prayer life. When we approach a holy God in prayer, we should always be quick to confess our sins. And God, out of His great love and mercy, will always forgive us (1 John 1:9). But we should not expect God's forgiveness for our sins if we, like the wicked servant in Jesus' parable, are hypocritically withholding forgiveness from others (Matthew 6:14–15).

As Jesus taught in Matthew 5:23–24, we should do whatever is necessary to make things right with others before we approach God in worship and prayer.

What can I do, right here, right now, to forgive someone who has wronged me?

A PLACE OF WORSHIP

*Do you not know that your body is the temple of
the Holy Spirit, who is in you, whom you have
from God, and you are not your own? For you
were bought with a price. Therefore glorify God in
your body and in your spirit, which are God's.*

1 Corinthians 6:19–20

For the ancient Corinthians, who were well-acquainted
with worship at idolatrous temples before coming to
Christ, Paul's exhortation in 1 Corinthians 6:19–20 (and
in 3:16–17) was surely transformative. Because God's Spirit
now lived inside them, the converted pagans could worship the one true God anywhere. Furthermore, they were
called to eschew heathen practices and use their bodies in
God-honoring ways.

How appropriate this message is for us today! Christ
purchased our salvation at great cost—His life—to transform
us into living temples of the Lord God Almighty. We are
vessels of worship. Therefore, every part of our body, from
head to toe, should be used to glorify our great Redeemer.

**What can I do, right here,
right now, to offer the living temple
of my body in worship to God?**

ALL THINGS FOR GOOD

We know that all things work together for
good to those who love God, to those who are
the called according to His purpose.

ROMANS 8:28

In life, we often struggle to choose a path forward when the road ahead is veiled in a fog of mystery. Yet Romans 8:28 provides one of the greatest assurances in scripture: If you are God's child, He works all things—even the painful, terrible, anxiety-producing, and mistake-filled things—for your good.

Verses 29–30 give assurance of this: "For those whom He foreknew, He also predestined to be conformed to the image of His Son, that He might be the firstborn among many brothers. Moreover those whom He predestined, He also called, and those whom He called, He also justified, and those whom He justified, He also glorified."

If you are God's child, your life is part of one glorious, unbreakable chain of joys, pains, and experiences that He planned for your ultimate, eternal good. He knows your past, present, and future. He determined it all. Rest in this.

What can I do, right here, right now,
to cling to the truth of Romans 8:28?

BEARING THE NAME

The disciples were first called Christians in Antioch.
ACTS 11:26

✠

Founded by Seleucus I Nicator, one of Alexander the Great's generals, Antioch was the third greatest city in the Roman Empire—both in size and importance—behind Rome and Alexandria by the first century AD. In God's sovereignty, Christianity had come to this influential trade-route town when Stephen's martyrdom incited persecution and scattered the Jerusalem church (Acts 11:19).

Barnabas and Paul helped establish the fledgling congregation in Antioch (Acts 11:22–26), and before long, the Antioch believers earned the moniker *Christians*, thus identifying them as a unique group of people within Greco-Roman society. In a morally depraved city, they stood out as different.

The word *Christian* means "Christ follower," or "of the party of Christ." Does your church stand out as unique in your city amid the moral depravity of modern culture? Do you?

Jesus' church bears His name. May He give us the grace and strength to represent Him well.

What can I do, right here, right now, to stand out uniquely as a Christ follower in today's world?

AN UNLIKELY MATCH
MADE IN HEAVEN

Count it all joy when you fall into various temptations,
knowing this, that the testing of your faith works
patience. But let patience have its perfect work, that
you may be perfect and complete, lacking nothing.

JAMES 1:2–4

Here are a few things that don't seem to go together well in life: swimming and sharks; bills and bankruptcy; rush-hour traffic and early-morning meetings; trials and joy.

Yet James 1 says that the mixture of trials and joy is not only possible, but ideal. But how? How can we have joy in the midst of great temptations and trials?

It's all about perspective.

God doesn't expect us to look forward to hardships or enjoy pain. Rather, He's calling us to a greater understanding of how He works in our lives. We can have joy in trials by knowing that God works all things—even great adversity—for our good (Romans 8:28). Trials build our faith. Trials develop godly character. Trials ultimately make us more like Him.

And that, after all, is the goal.

What can I do, right here, right now,
to find joy in the sanctification of trials?

EVIL TO GOOD

*"As for you, you thought evil against me,
but God meant it for good, to bring to pass,
as it is this day, to save many people alive."*

GENESIS 50:20

✚

Let's hope your siblings are nothing like the ones Joseph had.

Filled with jealousy and rage over their father's favoritism toward Joseph, Jacob's older sons banded together against Joseph, throwing him into a pit, selling him into slavery, and covering their wickedness with outrageous lies. More than a decade later, when they unexpectedly came face-to-face with Joseph, who had become the second-most powerful man in Egypt, they were terrified.

But Joseph saw the bigger picture: God had used the brothers' wicked scheming as part of a greater plan to position Joseph to save God's chosen people—the same nation through whom the Savior of the world would come.

God's plans are always bigger than we can see. What might look like evil to you now, God sovereignly means for your good.

Every time.

What can I do, right here, right now, to trust in God's sovereignty in the midst of evil?

NOT WHAT WE DESERVED

He has not dealt with us according to our sins
or rewarded us according to our iniquities.

PSALM 103:10

Is there a more beautiful verse in scripture than Psalm 103:10? What an amazing truth! What an encouraging reminder! What a source of joy and worship!

We deal with people according to their sins all the time. Too often, we lack grace, compassion, and patience when dealing with others' faults. We become angry, bitter, and prideful. We snap back. We remind the other person of all their previous wrongs against us. We give the cold shoulder. We hold grudges.

But not God. Were He to deal with us according to our sins, we would be eternally condemned, without hope. Instead, He shows us mercy and forgiveness. He rewards our meager faith and repentance with lavish love. "The LORD is gracious and full of compassion, slow to anger and great in mercy" (Psalm 145:8).

What a great God we serve!

**What can I do, right here, right now,
to show the love of God to those
who have sinned against me?**

FULLY SUFFICIENT

*All scripture is given by inspiration of God and is
profitable for doctrine, for reproof, for correction,
for instruction in righteousness, that the man of God
may be perfect, thoroughly furnished for all good works.*
2 TIMOTHY 3:16–17

✚

Imagine a mile-long bridge over a bay. It's 99 percent complete, with only fifty feet left unfinished in the middle. If cars were allowed to travel that bridge, those measly fifty feet would make all the difference. That bridge wouldn't be sufficient!

God has not given us merely a partial revelation of Himself, His salvation plan, and what He expects of us, creating a gap in knowledge and faith for us to perilously fall through. No! In scripture, God has graciously revealed *everything* we need to know in life—100 percent. The Bible is fully sufficient for our lives.

God's Word won't tell you the answer to every decision in life—for example, what job you should take. But where the Bible isn't direct, it offers guiding principles to be used with godly wisdom. Embrace its sufficiency for your life.

What can I do, right here, right now, to see the Bible as fully sufficient for all aspects of my life?

FAITHFUL GOD,
FAITH-FILLED PEOPLE

*"Therefore know that the L*ORD *your God,*
He is God, the faithful God who keeps covenant
and mercy to a thousand generations with those
who love Him and keep His commandments."

DEUTERONOMY 7:9

As we saw in our study of Ephesians 2:8–9 (page 27), God not only requires faith for our salvation, but He miraculously supplies it by regenerating our spiritually dead hearts to gospel truth. In this way, we are fully indebted to God for saving faith.

But God gets even more credit. Our faith rests solely and exclusively on God's faithfulness to us. If God were finite, imperfect, vindictive, or capricious in any way, our faith would crumble. If God ever suffered occasional lapses in judgment, wasn't completely honest, or broke a promise every so often, our faith would be meaningless.

But God is perfectly faithful. He is holy, righteous, and true. He always keeps His word. His love for His children never fails.

Our faith is secure because of our perfectly faithful God.

**What can I do, right here, right now,
to rest in God's faithfulness?**

FIGHTING ON YOUR KNEES

"Do not lead us into temptation, but deliver us from evil."
MATTHEW 6:13

✚

When Sennacherib, the ruthless ruler of the Assyrian Empire, arrived at Jerusalem with a massive army in 701 BC, he sent a threatening message to Judah's king, Hezekiah: Surrender or be destroyed.

Hezekiah rushed into the temple, spread out Sennacherib's letter, and cried out to God. That very night, God struck down 185,000 Assyrian warriors, causing Sennacherib to retreat (2 Kings 18–19 and Isaiah 36–37).

Chances are, there's no merciless army outside your door. But we as Christians are most definitely involved in battle— a spiritual one. Like Hezekiah, we would be wise to engage in it through prayer.

The weapons of our warfare are not physical, but spiritual. Through prayer, we meet the enemy head-on, fighting temptation, "pulling down. . .strongholds, casting down imaginations and every haughty thing that exalts itself against the knowledge of God, and bringing into captivity every thought to the obedience of Christ" (2 Corinthians 10:4–5).

Christian warriors fight on their knees.

**What can I do, right here, right now,
to prayerfully engage in spiritual warfare?**

BODY TALK

For this is the will of God, even your sanctification,
that you should abstain from fornication.

1 THESSALONIANS 4:3

When the New Testament authors wrote to first-century churches, their audiences were living in a sexually perverse world. Pagan religions conveniently sanctioned immorality as part of their practices. Temple prostitution abounded. Infidelity was rampant. Debauchery was everywhere.

The times and methods may have changed, but the problem has not. Modern-day pop culture glorifies promiscuity. Inappropriate advertising bombards us. Pornography is only a click away.

Yet God calls His children to be different. In fact, few topics receive more attention in scripture than sexual purity.

While all other sins are "outside the body" (1 Corinthians 6:18), sexual immorality violates one's own body, which was redeemed by the blood of Christ and transformed into the dwelling place of God's Spirit. Those who willfully and continually disobey God in this manner will be barred from His eternal presence (1 Corinthians 6:9; Ephesians 5:5; Revelation 21:8). Christians must put fornication to death (Colossians 3:5).

What can I do, right here, right now,
to honor the Lord with my body?

DOES GOD CHANGE HIS MIND?

*"I am God, and there is no one like Me, declaring
the end from the beginning and from ancient times
the things that are not yet done, saying, 'My counsel
shall stand, and I will do all My pleasure.'"*

ISAIAH 46:9–10

When King Saul disobeyed God's express command in
1 Samuel 15, it presented what appears to be—at least
initially—a theological conundrum. God said, "I regret that
I have set up Saul to be king" (verse 11). We see similar
language in Genesis 6:6 and Jonah 3:10.

Can God truly regret His decisions or change His
mind? If so, what does that mean for us as we consider
our purpose and God's providence?

To be clear: God's regret is not human regret. Though
He grieves over human sin (Genesis 6:6) and responds to
human repentance (Jonah 3:10), He doesn't make mistakes.
Plan A—God's only plan—is always in effect.

God genuinely engages with human choices. But
He will accomplish all His sovereign purposes that were
planned in eternity past.

**What can I do, right here, right now,
to make right choices while trusting
in God's overall providence?**

ATTACKING HELL

*"On this rock I will build My church,
and the gates of hell shall not prevail against it."*
MATTHEW 16:18

When Jesus predicted the rise and enduring power of His church—the worldwide fellowship of believers—to His disciples, He guaranteed "the gates of hell shall not prevail against it."

In ancient times, every important city protected itself with large gated walls. Gates were used for defense, not offense. It's interesting, then, that Jesus used city gates in this metaphorical picture of our enduring spiritual warfare.

God's church has certainly been under attack from Satan and his hellish forces for two thousand years. But if we're doing our job properly, we must also be on the spiritual offensive, storming the gates of hell, "casting down imaginations and every haughty thing that exalts itself against the knowledge of God" (2 Corinthians 10:5).

As believers, led by God's Spirit, we must take the fight to the enemy's gates. Satan will not prevail. Our victory is sure in Christ!

**What can I do, right here, right now,
to join the church's fight against evil?**

JOY IN HIS PRESENCE

Glory and honor are in His presence;
strength and gladness are in His place.

1 CHRONICLES 16:27

✚

Here's a definite from ancient Israel: There ain't no party like an ark of the covenant party!

Near the beginning of his reign, King David held a grand ceremony to usher the ark into Jerusalem, calling "all Israel" (1 Chronicles 15:3) to attend. Thousands of people lined the streets and sang praise songs, including a psalm of David specifically written for the occasion (1 Chronicles 16:7–36) as musicians belted out tunes. David even busted some dance moves. What a scene it must have been!

Then and now, to be in the presence of God is to experience great joy. This will be indescribably true in heaven, but it's also gloriously true right here, right now.

To experience God's strength and gladness, enter into His holy presence. Seek Him in His Word. Talk to Him in prayer. Listen to His Spirit inside you. Worship Him among His people. (And if the Spirit moves, dance!)

**What can I do, right here, right now,
to experience the joy of God's presence?**

THE END GAME OF TRIBULATIONS

We also glory in tribulations, knowing that
tribulation works patience, and patience experience,
and experience hope. And hope does not make us
ashamed, because the love of God has been poured out
in our hearts by the Holy Spirit who was given to us.
ROMANS 5:3–5

Patience. Experience. Hope. Who doesn't want more of
these? Clearly, our lives improve as we mature in each of
them and enjoy their benefits.

Yet in God's economy, we gain patience, experience,
and hope through a means none of us would willingly
choose on our own: tribulations.

Nothing accelerates our spiritual maturation process
like hardships. Only then do we truly begin to trust in
something—or someone—other than ourselves and our
world. When other earthly blessings are stripped away
and our eyes turn to God, His Spirit will develop more
patience, experience, and hope in us.

Knowing this, we can "glory in tribulations" because
we begin to understand their glorious, eternal purpose.

What can I do, right here, right now,
to acknowledge and appreciate the
end game of tribulations?

SON OF GOD

*In the beginning was the Word, and the Word was
with God, and the Word was God. The same was in the
beginning with God. All things were made by Him,
and without Him nothing was made that was made.*

JOHN 1:1–3

When it comes to the subject of Jesus' divinity and eternal
nature, the title "Son of God" has tripped up plenty of
people over the centuries. One such man was Arius, who
lived in the fourth century AD.

Arius misunderstood this title and promoted the fallacious idea that Jesus was God the Father's first creation. Not
true! Passages such as John 1:1–3, Romans 9:5, Hebrews
1:8, Titus 2:13, and 2 Peter 1:1 all affirm Jesus' full deity
and eternality.

This is of vital theological importance. Nothing created can save us from sin or be worthy of our worship. Yet
because the eternal Son of God is both fully God and fully
man, He was able to perfectly fulfill the role of our Savior.
Thank You, Lord Jesus!

**What can I do, right here, right now, to better
understand Jesus' divinity and eternality?**

MYSTERIES REVEALED, SECRETS KEPT

"The secret things belong to the LORD our God, but those things that are revealed belong to us and to our children forever, so that we may do all the words of this law."

DEUTERONOMY 29:29

While the Bible is fully sufficient for our lives (see page 62), it doesn't answer all our deepest questions about the human experience or every minute detail of theology.

What was God doing in eternity past? How did the incarnation happen? What will heaven be like? How does the Trinity work?

While the Bible sheds some light on these questions—and many other mind-benders—it also leaves many perplexing realities shrouded in mystery.

And that's okay. God is God, and we are not. In His infinite wisdom, He has chosen to reveal much—but not all—of Himself and His ways to us. He has revealed enough. In that gap, we must learn to trust Him and be faithful with what He *has* given us.

What can I do, right here, right now, to rest in what God has revealed to me?

THE PRAYER OF STRUGGLING FAITH

Immediately the father of the child cried out and said with tears, "Lord, I believe; help my unbelief."

MARK 9:24

✚

Shortly after His transfiguration, Jesus met a man with a demon-possessed son. The man was desperate because the demon was slowly destroying the boy.

"If You can do anything, have compassion on us and help us," the father pleaded (Mark 9:22).

Jesus paused. The word *if* was a problem.

"If you can believe," He responded, "all things are possible to him who believes" (Mark 9:23).

The father got the point. "Lord, I believe," he said. "Help my unbelief."

God requires our faith for salvation. But he also knows we are weak and imperfect. He understands we have good days and bad days. He knows human faith vacillates.

Are you struggling today to trust the Lord in whatever challenges you're facing? Just like the father did in Mark 9, ask Jesus to strengthen your faltering faith. In the midst of your struggles, cry out to God, "Lord, I believe! Help my unbelief!"

What can I do, right here, right now, to overcome my unbelief with God's help?

POSTURE AND POWER

*"All things, whatever you ask in prayer,
believing, you shall receive."*

MATTHEW 21:22

Imagine having all the power in the universe at your disposal. Imagine being able to access the strength that keeps the sun shining, the planets spinning, and human hearts beating.

Well, if you are a follower of Christ, you do.

Of course, we humans can't do anything on our own. We are finite, frail, and fraught with sin. But through Christ, we have access—through prayer—to all the power of Lord God Almighty, ruler of heaven and earth.

We must be careful here, though. God is not our personal genie or divine butler. Prayer is not rubbing a magic lamp or ringing a bell for service. Our prayerful posture should be, *"Your* kingdom come. *Your* will be done" (Matthew 6:10, emphases added). Not ours.

Still, God wants us—with desires that match His—to ask Him for much in faith. And when we ask according to His will, we will see His kingdom advance in unimaginable ways (James 5:16).

**What can I do, right here, right now,
to desire and ask for what God desires?**

THE FORTRESS OF GODLY DISCIPLINE

He who has no rule over his own spirit is like a city that is broken down and without walls.

PROVERBS 25:28

✚

In the ancient world, when there was no such thing as an "Iron Dome" missile defense system or multibillion-dollar warships patrolling coastlines, stone city walls were the best protection against enemy forces. Without protective walls, city inhabitants were vulnerable to attack.

It's this imagery that Proverbs 25:28 speaks to. But in this picture, the city wall is likened to something surprising: personal discipline.

Self-discipline, or "rule over [one's] own spirit" is like a strong barricade against invading temptations and harmful spiritual forces. The more personal discipline we build with God's help, the more we will be able to repel spiritual attacks.

How do we achieve this disciplined wall of defense? Godly decision-making is built with the bricks of biblical truth and the mortar of prayer, buttressed by the wise counsel found within godly fellowship.

What can I do, right here, right now, to build self-discipline?

BEFORE TIME BEGAN

*He has chosen us in Him before the foundation
of the world, that we should be holy and without
blame before Him in love, having predestined us to
the adoption of children by Jesus Christ to Himself,
according to the good pleasure of His will.*

EPHESIANS 1:4–5

When we consider our purpose and how to discern God's will for our lives, it's so easy to become nearsighted, focusing keenly on the here and now while allowing the big picture to get fuzzy. Perhaps no passage in scripture can help cure our spiritual myopia like Ephesians 1:4–5.

Rest in this truth, friend: Before you were born—even before time began—God chose you to be "holy and without blame before Him." Before God created the universe, He knew you. Before Genesis 1:1, He had chosen to adopt you into His eternal family. Before He said, "Let there be light," He purposed to bring you into the sunshine of Christ's love.

What can give you more purpose than that?

**What can I do, right here, right now,
to bask in the beauty of God's sovereign love?**

TEMPERATURE CHECK

*"I know your works, that you are neither cold nor
hot. I wish that you were cold or hot. So then,
because you are lukewarm, and neither cold nor
hot, I will spew you out of My mouth."*

REVELATION 3:15–16

✛

The ancient city of Laodicea in Asia Minor (modern-day
Turkey) was renowned for many things, including its public
water system. A remarkable aqueduct system piped in water
from hot springs nearly five miles away. But by the time
the water reached Laodicea, it was likely tepid and laden
with mineral deposits.

Perhaps this is what Jesus was referring to analogously
in Revelation 3:15–16. Some commentators, however,
believe this passage pictures the Laodicean church as an
unhospitable host for the Lord. Either way, the message
is clear: Jesus has no use for a lukewarm church.

What's the spiritual temperature of your church?
What's *your* spiritual temperature? Are you contributing a
lukewarm apathy toward your congregation, or an infectious
fire for God's kingdom?

**What can I do, right here, right now,
to help my church be fully devoted to Christ?**

THE STRENGTH OF JOY

*"Do not be sorrowful, for the joy of
the LORD is your strength."*

NEHEMIAH 8:10

Incredibly, Nehemiah had finished rebuilding Jerusalem's wall in only fifty-two days. On the first day of the Feast of Trumpets, the entire group of returned Jewish exiles—more than forty-two thousand people—gathered near the Water Gate. There, Ezra, the priest, read the Law of Moses to the congregation. And the people wept.

The returned exiles realized how far they had fallen short of God's commands. Yet Nehemiah quickly stemmed the flow of sadness. "Do not be sorrowful," he said, "for the joy of the LORD is your strength!"

Godly sorrow and repentance is an appropriate response to sin (2 Corinthians 7:10). But we aren't meant to linger there forever. Rather, "if we confess our sins, He is faithful and just to forgive us our sins and to cleanse us from all unrighteousness" (1 John 1:9). Knowing this glorious gospel truth, we can enter the joy of the Lord, which gives us strength.

**What can I do, right here, right now, to
experience the strength of joy in my salvation?**

A DEFEATED FOE

*Be sober, be vigilant, because your adversary the
devil walks about like a roaring lion, seeking whom
he may devour. Resist him, steadfast in the faith.*

1 PETER 5:8–9

Beginning in the Age of Enlightenment (an ironic descrip-
tion from a spiritual perspective!) in the seventeenth and
eighteenth centuries, humanity began to seriously doubt
the invisible. If something couldn't be proven empirically,
the thinking went, it wasn't real.

The fallout from this drastic shift toward humanism
still lingers today. Spiritual truths are questioned, and
members of the unseen realm, such as angels, demons, and
Satan, are quickly dismissed.

But scripture is quite clear: There *is* a spiritual realm,
and Satan is a real being who is diametrically opposed
to God. In trials, we must be sober-minded and vigilant,
always aware that God's age-old (and ultimately doomed)
enemy is looking to attack us in weak moments.

So resist Satan in prayer. Withstand him through faith.
Defy him with the power of God's Word and the blood
of Jesus' cross. Through Christ, the Christian's victory has
already been won, and Satan is a conquered foe.

**What can I do, right here,
right now, to resist Satan's attacks?**

WITHOUT SIN

For He has made Him who knew no sin to be sin for us,
that we might be made the righteousness of God in Him.

2 CORINTHIANS 5:21

Perfection is elusive in our fallen world. Our bodies need doctors. Our cars need mechanics. And no major league batter has ever come close to batting 1.000 over a full season.

Our spiritual lives are no different. We all join the apostle Paul in lamenting, "For I do not do the good that I want, but I do the evil that I do not want" (Romans 7:19). For these reasons, perfection seems like an utterly foreign concept to us.

Yet Jesus, the eternal Son of God, was perfect in every way. He was "in all points tempted as we are, yet without sin" (Hebrews 4:15).

This is astounding! And it's why Jesus—and only Jesus—was able to fulfill our role as Savior. Only a sinless sacrifice would be acceptable to God on our behalf. Jesus is that sacrifice.

What can I do, right here, right now,
to better appreciate Jesus' sinless sacrifice?

WORDS OF ETERNITY

"The grass withers, the flower fades,
but the word of our God shall stand forever."

ISAIAH 40:8

History is littered with memorable quotes. "I have a dream" (Martin Luther King Jr. in an August 28, 1963 speech in Washington, D.C.); "To be or not to be—that is the question" (Hamlet in William Shakespeare's *Hamlet*); "Ask not what your country can do for you—ask what you can do for your country" (US President John F. Kennedy in his inaugural address on January 20, 1961); "Whoa" (actor Keanu Reeves in every movie he's ever done).

Okay, scratch that last one. But you get the point. Meaningful words have staying power. Nothing, though, will last forever like God's Word.

Human words—even the greatest—have a shelf life. But the words of the eternal God will endure forever.

This gives us great hope. What was true when Moses chiseled stone, when David penned songs, and when Paul authored letters is still true today. Praise God for His enduring Word!

**What can I do, right here, right now,
to spend more time in God's eternal Word?**

MUSTARD-SEED FAITH

"If you have faith like a grain of mustard seed, you shall say to this mountain, 'Move from here to a distant place,' and it shall move, and nothing shall be impossible for you."

MATTHEW 17:20

✠

After Jesus healed a demon-possessed boy (see page 72), the disciples asked the Lord why they hadn't been able to cast out the evil spirit themselves. Jesus replied plainly, "Because of your unbelief" (Matthew 17:20). He then shared one of His most well-known metaphors on faith and prayer.

Jesus told the Twelve that with faith the size of a mustard seed—smaller than a grain of rice—they could figuratively move mountains.

God doesn't *need* our faith and prayers to act, and He's not looking for "faith experts." In His sovereign love and providence, He uses the relatively small faith of imperfect people to accomplish great things.

Want to move mountains? Wherever you're at in life, however big or small your faith is, approach God humbly and expectantly, and watch Him move in mighty ways.

What can I do, right here, right now, to pray in faith?

THE GOD WHO HEARS

The LORD has heard my supplication;
the LORD will receive my prayer.

PSALM 6:9

Human communication is tricky.

Calls drop. We get put on hold. Video conference feeds lag. Kids don't always listen to their parents. Those who are hearing-impaired can't always understand what's being spoken. Emotions can cloud our clarity. Language barriers can hinder us. We interrupt and get interrupted. And the message we intend isn't always the message that's received.

Aren't you glad that communication with God isn't like that? God *always* hears our prayers perfectly. He is always listening to the praises, confessions, requests, and pleas of His children. He loves hearing from us and acting for our good.

When you pray, remember that your Father in heaven is listening. He hears. He cares. And He will answer in His providence and timing.

So we exult with King David, who wrote in Psalm 40:1: "I waited patiently for the LORD, and He inclined to me and heard my cry."

What can I do, right here, right now, to grow in confidence that God truly does hear my prayers?

ESCAPE PLAN

The Lord knows how to deliver the
godly out of temptations.

2 PETER 2:9

Schoolkids do drills to help them learn how to escape a
burning building. Flight attendants point out exit doors
before takeoff in case of an emergency. And Hollywood
certainly has a thing for prison escapes, giving us films such
as *Escape from Alcatraz*, *Escape from New York*, *The Great
Escape*, and that pinnacle of cinematic achievement, *Escape
from the Planet of the Apes*.

For Christians, the greatest danger we need to escape
isn't Nazis, Soviets, or power-hungry prison wardens. It's
sin. But when temptation calls, we are never trapped
behind bars. God knows how to deliver the godly out of
temptations.

So call out to Him. Listen to His Spirit. Remember
His Word. Obey His commands. And He will reveal the
escape plan.

**What can I do, right here, right now,
to seek God in the midst of temptation?**

THE GOOD PURPOSES OF GOD

"I know the thoughts that I think toward you," says the LORD, "thoughts of peace and not of evil, to give you an expected end."

JEREMIAH 29:11

The year was 597 BC. King Nebuchadnezzar had just deported the second major wave of Jewish exiles from Judah to Babylon. Writing from Jerusalem, the prophet Jeremiah sent his former countrymen a letter, telling them to trust in the Lord as they awaited the fulfillment of His promise to bring His people home.

The message of Jeremiah 29:11 was given specifically to the Jewish exiles of the sixth century BC, but God's heart toward His children today is no different. His thoughts toward us are of "peace and not of evil." Even in the great hardships of life, He sovereignly works them for our good (Romans 8:28).

If you are God's child through faith in Christ, He is for you, not against you. His purpose for you is good—even if often unseen and mysterious—and He will bring it to its expected end.

What can I do, right here, right now, to trust in the good purposes of God?

SPIRIT OF GENEROSITY

Nor was there anyone among them who lacked, for as
many as were possessors of lands or houses sold them, and
brought the proceeds of the things that were sold, and
laid them down at the apostles' feet. And distribution
was made to every man according to his need.

ACTS 4:34–35

The early church can teach us a thing or two about generosity.

As Christianity began in Jerusalem, the new believers pooled their resources to meet each other's needs. They faithfully preached God's Word while also feeding poor widows (Acts 6:1–7). They took up offerings to assist distant congregations (2 Corinthians 8–9). They financially supported and opened their homes to traveling Christian workers (3 John 5–8). Imagine if we too, in our multimillion-dollar sanctuaries, had this spirit of generosity!

Does your church actively help the needy? Does it robustly support missions work locally and abroad? Does it minister to the needs of sister churches?

A healthy, God-fearing church cares for the needs of others.

What can I do, right here, right now, to cultivate a spirit of generosity in myself and my church?

THE ASSURANCE OF
JOY UNSPEAKABLE

*Though now you do not see Him, yet believing, you rejoice
with joy unspeakable and full of glory, receiving the
result of your faith, even the salvation of your souls.*

1 PETER 1:8–9

Some things in life are merely a wish, a dream, a longing for something to be: that elusive job promotion, lingering debts to finally be overcome, or freedom from hurt that others have caused.

They are unrealized desires—things currently unseen that we hope will one day come true.

Then we come to 1 Peter 1:8–9 and read about something else unseen. But this is different. *Way* different.

We have never seen Jesus, and yet through "believing" we can "rejoice with joy unspeakable" because we know we will see Him.

You might not ever get that job promotion, debt-free living, or freedom from emotional hurts in this life. But through faith in Jesus, you can experience unspeakable joy both now and in eternity as you rejoice in the salvation of your coming Savior.

**What can I do, right here, right now,
to experience unspeakable joy in Jesus?**

THE NEARNESS OF GOD

The Lord is at hand.

PHILIPPIANS 4:5

Philippians 4:6–7 is a wonderful passage to remember in trials. It sets a high bar—"Be anxious for nothing" (verse 6)—then tells us that prayer is the key to achieving "the peace of God, which passes all understanding" (verse 7).

But these glorious realities are only possible because of the often overlooked truth in the preceding verse: "The Lord is at hand"—meaning, He is near.

We can have freedom from anxiety because the Lord is at hand. We can experience the peace of God amidst trials because the Lord is at hand. We can offer thanksgiving amid suffering because the Lord is at hand. Our hearts and minds can be guarded from evil because the Lord is at hand.

Our God is not distant or aloof. He cares (1 Peter 5:7). He is near, "a very present help in trouble" (Psalm 46:1). He graciously indwells His people with His Spirit, giving us access to the very power that raised Jesus from the dead (Romans 8:11).

The Lord is at hand!

What can I do, right here, right now, to remember God's active nearness?

SACRIFICE OF ATONEMENT

Now He has appeared once at the end of the world
to put away sin by the sacrifice of Himself.
Hebrews 9:26

Being a cow or sheep or goat in ancient Israel was quite a dangerous affair. If you didn't become the family dinner, you were likely headed to the sacrificial altar.

The amount of animals sacrificed under the Old Testament law was staggering. When King Solomon dedicated God's temple, he offered "twenty-two thousand oxen and a hundred and twenty thousand sheep" (1 Kings 8:63). Thousands more animals were offered in the temple sacrifices each year. That's a lot of cheeseburgers and lamb chops.

All these offerings were to temporarily atone for the sins of God's people until He provided a perfect sacrifice (Hebrews 10:14). That sacrifice is Jesus! He is the true "Lamb of God who takes away the sin of the world" (John 1:29).

Through His perfect obedience to God's law, Jesus became the once-for-all atoning sacrifice for our sins, making us right with God through faith in Him.

What can I do, right here, right now, to worship Jesus as my perfect, atoning sacrifice?

PROPER SWORD USE

Take the helmet of salvation and the sword
of the Spirit, which is the word of God.

EPHESIANS 6:17

God's heart is grieved when humans use the sword of the Spirit to fight the wrong battles. Some use the Bible to insult other religions, enslave ethnicities, subjugate the weak, propagate destructive heresies, and destroy relationships over differing points of theology.

God's Word is a mighty weapon, yes, but it isn't to be used for such things. Instead, it's for teaching, correcting, and training in righteousness (2 Timothy 3:16–17), spiritual growth (1 Peter 2:2), guidance and encouragement (Psalm 119:105), strength against temptation (119:11), and revealing God and His plan for salvation (Romans 15:4). The sword of the Spirit, part of the overall "armor of God," is for standing against the devil's schemes (Ephesians 6:11), battling against spiritual forces rather than "flesh and blood" (verse 12).

May we never wield scripture carelessly or pridefully. It's not the sword of destruction or personal ambition. It's the "sword of the Spirit."

What can I do, right here, right now,
to humbly take up the sword of the Spirit?

FAITH-BUILDING FAITH

For I long to see you, that I may impart some spiritual
gift to you, to the end you may be established—
that is, that I may be comforted together with
you by the mutual faith of both you and me.

ROMANS 1:11–12

✚

Few things in life are as encouraging as witnessing the powerful faith of another believer. Of course, we marvel at the amazing faith of biblical saints such as Abraham, Moses, Daniel, and Paul. We get inspired by more recent pillars of faith such as Martin Luther, Charles Spurgeon, Billy Graham, and R. C. Sproul.

But perhaps most meaningful are the examples of faith by people we know personally: the young widower with three kids, the couple who continues to trust God even after losing a child, the senior saint who continues to serve. The everyday faith of others builds our own.

Are you encouraged by the faith of fellow believers in your life? Are you seeking to encourage others as you live out your own faith?

What can I do, right here, right now,
to mutually build up others' faith?

ANYWHERE, ANYTIME

"O Lord, I beseech You, let Your ear now be attentive to the prayer of Your servant."

NEHEMIAH 1:11

Nehemiah was a man of prayer. That's clear from his biblical story. But look closer and you'll notice a pattern: Nehemiah believed in spur-of-the-moment prayers.

When Nehemiah heard that Jerusalem's walls remained broken generations after the Babylonian destruction, he prayed (Nehemiah 1:4). When the Persian king, Artaxerxes, asked what was troubling him, Nehemiah prayed (2:4). When he learned of a plot to harm him and his wall-rebuilding efforts, Nehemiah prayed (4:9; 6:9). When he pursued spiritual reforms, Nehemiah prayed (13:14, 22, 31).

Nehemiah didn't wait until he had a quiet half hour to seek God's face. He often prayed on the spot wherever he was, whatever the need.

Our prayers shouldn't be limited to Sunday church services or the quietness of our bedrooms. Through prayer, you have access to the God of heaven anytime, anywhere. Call out to Him. He is always there.

What can I do, right here, right now, to pray throughout the day?

HELP NEEDED

But the fruit of the Spirit is love, joy,
peace, long-suffering, gentleness,
goodness, faith, meekness, self-control.
GALATIANS 5:22–23

No doubt about it: God wants us to have self-control.

The apostle Paul wrote that "every man who strives for victory has self-control in all things" (1 Corinthians 9:25). Paul instructed church leaders to practice self-control (1 Timothy 3:2–3), and he said the same for Christian men and women (Titus 2:2, 5). Peter said self-control was essential for a strong prayer life (1 Peter 4:7). And of course, self-control is a "fruit of the Spirit" (Galatians 5:23).

And therein lies the rub. Self-control is not something we can self-generate. We need the help of God's Spirit. We can grow in self-control and show more of it as we make good decisions and choose love in our actions and words. But we can't have it apart from God's work in our hearts.

Want more self-control? Pray for more of God's Spirit.

What can I do, right here, right now,
to develop more self-control?

ALL FOR HIS GLORY

*Whether you eat or drink, or whatever
you do, do all for the glory of God.*

1 CORINTHIANS 10:31

Scripture is abundantly clear: For all born-again believers, God's glory must be our main purpose in life. In Isaiah 43:7, God mentions "everyone who is called by My name, for I have created him for My glory."

Then we naturally ask, *Well, yes, but how do I do that? What does glorifying God look like in my day-to-day life?* First Corinthians 10:31 gives us the key: We keep God's exaltation at the forefront of all we do—even the smallest, most mundane activities like eating and drinking. Give thanks for your meals; that glorifies God. Be honest and diligent at your job; that glorifies God. Give your time, energy, and money to advance His kingdom; that glorifies God. Love your family; that glorifies God. Watch what you say, do, look at, and think; that glorifies God.

Whatever you do, do it all for God's glory!

**What can I do, right here, right now,
to glorify God in my daily rhythms?**

EQUIPPED TO SERVE

*Since you are zealous of spiritual gifts, seek that
you may excel for the edification of the church.*

1 CORINTHIANS 14:12

✝

Nowhere in the Bible will you find a reference to 90-minute parishioners. These are folks who attend one service a week (or less) and leave immediately afterward. In and out...just like a fast-food drive-through.

Instead, our Christian fellowship should be marked by joyful worship and humble servanthood. God has equipped us to do this with the spiritual gifts He has provided to all believers. As Romans 12:6 says, we have "differing gifts according to the grace that is given to us."

So use your spiritual gifts to build the church. The goal isn't to produce a perfectly packaged Sunday morning experience that gets rave reviews on Yelp. It's to bring glory to God and edify the church (reread today's scripture).

When you walk through those church doors each week, be a giver, not a taker. Look for ways to serve and minister. Don't let your God-given gifts go to waste!

**What can I do, right here,
right now, to serve in my church?**

JOY IN THE MORNING

His anger endures but a moment;
in His favor is life. Weeping may endure for
a night, but joy comes in the morning.

PSALM 30:5

King David wrote Psalm 30 with an eye toward the future. According to the psalm's title, he created it for "the dedication of the house of David" (that is, the temple)—an event that occurred after his death (1 Kings 8). David was looking ahead.

This too must be our mindset in the midst of trials. While the pain of suffering is real, Psalm 30:5 reminds us that "joy comes in the morning."

But wait, you say. *I woke up today carrying the same burden I fell asleep with last night. Where is this morning joy?*

The words *night* and *morning* in Psalm 30:5 refer to periods of time, not necessarily a 24-hour span. Like David, we must look ahead in faith.

Take heart, friend. As sure as the morning sun rises, God's joy will come. He is faithful.

What can I do, right here,
right now, to trust in God for joy?

ANXIETY'S GREAT ENEMY

Be anxious for nothing, but in everything,
by prayer and supplication with thanksgiving,
let your requests be made known to God.

PHILIPPIANS 4:6

✚

Human anxiety is one of life's greatest challenges. It can feel overwhelming at times, like being stalked by a relentless predator or finding yourself trapped in an inescapable prison cell. But scripture offers hope in the midst of our worries: prayer.

Prayer isn't an enchanted potion or a rabbit's foot. It often doesn't even immediately solve the problem. But its efficacy is more powerful than any other remedy for anxiety.

That's because prayer gets to the root of human worry: fear and disbelief. When we worry, we're revealing our lack of faith in God's love, care, providence, and power. Worry leads to futile human efforts.

Prayer, however, is an acknowledgement that God can handle the situation even though we can't. Prayer is a confession that God is good, His promises are true, and He will help. Prayer is a display of faith, and as we present our concerns to God, our anxiety will slowly fade away.

What can I do, right here, right now,
to fight anxiety with prayer?

THE ONLY WAY

Jesus said to him, "I am the way, the truth, and the life. No man comes to the Father except through Me."
JOHN 14:6

Don't you love GPS apps?

Unlike the old days—when we'd spread out our biblical-scroll-length Rand McNally roadmaps across the steering wheel and attempt to read incredibly small print at seventy miles per hour while *not* ending up in a multi-car inferno—today's GPS navigation systems make driving to hitherto unknown parts a breeze. GPS even gives you multiple route options, showing the estimated time of travel for each one. Well done, global positioning satellites. Thank you.

While GPS offers many routes to the same destination, the same can't be said of heaven. There is only one way to God: through faith in His Son, Jesus Christ.

This is not a popular message. The world thinks it's arrogant, exclusionary, and misinformed. But Jesus made it very clear: We only come into a right relationship with our heavenly Father—forgiven, justified, and redeemed—through Him.

What can I do, right here, right now, to acknowledge Jesus as the only way to God?

TEMPTING. . .
BUT NO THANKS

Your word have I hidden in my heart,
that I might not sin against You.
PSALM 119:11

Even the best writers need guidelines to help them in their craft. (Ain't that the truth!) Book authors use the *Chicago Manual of Style*. Newspaper journalists (the few, the proud) use the *Associated Press Stylebook*. College students look to the *Modern Language Association Handbook*. And doctors. . .well, we're not actually sure what doctors use. But that's okay—we can't read their handwriting anyway.

Just like a style guide helps writers avoid mistakes, knowing the Bible helps Christians avoid sin. Only in God's Word do we find what God expects of us—His instructions, commands, and prohibitions. We can't know what our heavenly Father expects of us without reading His manual for life. The more we memorize scripture, the more divine resources we'll have on hand when temptations appear. His Word is truly life-giving.

What can I do, right here, right now,
to hide God's Word in my heart?

GROWING FAITH

He did not stagger at the promise of God through unbelief but was strong in faith, giving glory to God.

ROMANS 4:20

We often hold up Abraham as a paragon of faith. And rightfully so, considering Abraham, old and childless at the time, believed what probably sounded like an outlandish promise from God: that he would become the father of a great nation, through which God would bless the whole world.

But while Romans 4:20 and Hebrews 11 venerate Abraham's overall faith, it wasn't perfect. At various times, he laughed at God's promise (Genesis 17:17) and suggested an alternative option to God's plan (Genesis 15:2–3). Over time, though, Abraham truly believed God, and God "counted it to him for righteousness" (Genesis 15:6).

Abraham's faith was a living, growing entity. It ebbed and flowed, but trended in the right direction through the years.

This should be a great encouragement to us because our faith isn't perfect either. But it should grow over time. As you see God's continual faithfulness in your life, your faith should grow too.

What can I do, right here, right now, to choose to trust God?

A WISE PLAN

*"Now give me wisdom and knowledge, that I may
go out and come in before this people, for who can
judge this people of Yours, who are so great?"*

2 CHRONICLES 1:10

Imagine having a blank check from God. What would
you ask for? A new car? A new house? A new boss?
Good health? Financial security? Kids who aren't messy?
(Good luck with that.)

King Solomon asked for wisdom.

When Solomon began to rule Israel, God said to him,
"Ask what I shall give you" (2 Chronicles 1:7). Solomon,
realizing the great task before him, answered, "Give me
wisdom and knowledge." God honored that request, endow-
ing Solomon with "a wise and understanding heart" without
equal (1 Kings 3:12).

Those who are wise ask for more wisdom from God.
As Solomon wrote later in life, "If you cry after knowledge and lift up your voice for understanding,. . .you shall
understand the fear of the LORD and find the knowledge
of God" (Proverbs 2:3, 5).

Pray for God's wisdom often, and you will be blessed.

**What can I do, right here, right now,
to seek the wisdom of God?**

EYE TEST

I will set no wicked thing before my eyes.
PSALM 101:3

Sin takes God's good gifts and corrupts them in the most heinous of ways. Nowhere is this seen better than in the pornography industry.

Sex is a beautiful gift from God, designed for a husband and wife within the boundaries of marriage. Yet sin has twisted this great blessing in ways that are almost unimaginable. In the United States alone, some estimates figure pornography as a 100 billion-dollar-a-year business.

Do you struggle with pornography? Countless men do, whether Christians or not. But God calls us to something better. He calls us to cast off lust and pursue righteousness. He calls us to be holy as He is holy (1 Peter 1:16).

With prayer and accountability, guard your heart, control your desires, and watch your eyes, "bringing into captivity every thought to the obedience of Christ" (2 Corinthians 10:5).

What can I do, right here, right now, to honor God with my eyes?

PREPARED IN ADVANCE

*For we are His workmanship, created in Christ
Jesus for good works, which God has before
ordained that we should walk in them.*

EPHESIANS 2:10

*What should I do in life? Where should I work? How should
I build God's kingdom?*

Have you ever asked yourself any of these questions?
Of course, we all have. As we consider our path in life,
Ephesians 2:10 provides an amazing overview.

The word *For* that begins this remarkable verse alludes
to the apostle Paul's declaration in verses 8–9 that our
salvation is by grace through faith—all of which God
ordained in eternity past (Ephesians 1:4–5). Everything
about us as believers—including our faith, salvation, and
good works—is divinely decreed. By His grace, God works
in us and through us to advance the gospel.

Your salvation and the good works that follow were
planned in ages past. You might not know all the minute
details yet. But God does. He ordained it before time began.

**What can I do, right here, right now,
to perform the good works that God
has prepared in advance for me?**

A FALSE GOSPEL

*"Take heed and beware of covetousness,
for a man's life does not consist in the
abundance of the things that he possesses."*

LUKE 12:15

Like a creeping virus, the prosperity gospel is a devious infection that has wormed its way into churches worldwide. Here are some of the prosperity gospel's tenets: God wants to bless you with health and wealth! Prosperity is your spiritual birthright! Material riches are a sign of God's favor upon you! Why would a loving God want us to be poor and sick? Name it and claim it!

Avoid the prosperity gospel at all costs. It binds our hearts to perishing things of this world rather than true spiritual riches in Christ. God has promised believers incredible spiritual blessings in this life and the next—but never earthly treasure.

The apostle Paul had sharp words for prosperity teachers and the "perverse disputes of men of corrupt minds and destitute of the truth, supposing that gain is godliness." His solution? "Withdraw yourself from such" (1 Timothy 6:5).

**What can I do, right here, right now, to have
a biblical view of health and wealth?**

RESTORING JOY

Restore to me the joy of Your salvation,
and uphold me with Your free Spirit.

PSALM 51:12

David had done the unthinkable.

Israel's great king had committed adultery with Bathsheba, and after finding out she was pregnant, he tried to cover up his sin by lying, deceiving, and ultimately arranging for her husband, Uriah, to be killed in battle. David's sin was atrocious, and when God sent the prophet Nathan to confront the king, he humbled himself and sought God's forgiveness. Psalm 51 is a reflection of David's beautiful, genuine repentance.

Christians are sinners saved by God's grace, becoming more like Him through His indwelling Spirit. Yet we still struggle with our old sinful nature. When you fall, cry out to the Lord like David did. Confess your sin and God will forgive you (1 John 1:9); He already has through Christ! Sin takes away our spiritual joy, so ask the Lord to restore the joy of your salvation. God is faithful. He will do it.

What can I do, right here,
right now, to experience the joy of
my salvation in repentance?

EXPERIENCING
THE PEACE OF GOD

And the peace of God, which passes all understanding,
shall guard your hearts and minds through Christ Jesus.

PHILIPPIANS 4:7

The ancient Romans were known for saying, "If you want peace, prepare for war." That's a pretty ironic statement coming from an empire that "devoured and broke in pieces [other nations] and trampled the remainder with its feet" (Daniel 7:7).

Humanity has always longed for peace, but conflict has touched every corner of the earth since the fall. It's remarkable, then, that scripture promises believers "the peace of God."

This peace is altogether different than worldly peace. It cannot be secured with military might or human striving. This peace is linked closely to trust, contentment, and faithful perseverance in trials. It's a calming assurance that God truly does have our good in mind and is actively present in all situations. It's a spiritual quietness of the soul in those who cast their cares on Him.

You too can have this peace by seeking the Lord in prayer.

**What can I do, right here, right now,
to rest in the "peace of God"?**

OUR GREAT HIGH PRIEST

Since then we have a great high priest who
has passed into the heavens, Jesus, the Son
of God, let us hold fast our profession.
HEBREWS 4:14

✚

For centuries, the ancient Jews worshipped God—from a distance.

In the tabernacle and later the temple, a massive curtain separated the public places of worship from the Most Holy Place, where God's presence dwelt. Only the high priest—once a year, on the Day of Atonement—could enter the sacred inner chamber to sacrifice on behalf of the people. Even before he entered, the high priest had to undergo an elaborate ritual to ceremonially purify himself.

The message was clear: Sinful humanity cannot approach a holy God without an unstained mediator.

Through His perfect life, atoning death, and miraculous resurrection, Jesus has become that mediator—our great High Priest. When He died, the temple curtain was torn in two, signaling the era of the new covenant through Christ's blood. Now He continually intercedes on behalf of His people at God's right hand. Thank You, Jesus!

What can I do, right here, right now,
to approach God through Christ?

ALWAYS PURPOSEFUL, ALWAYS SUCCESSFUL

"So shall My word be that goes out of My mouth. It shall not return to Me void, but it shall accomplish what I please and it shall prosper in the thing for which I sent it."

ISAIAH 55:11

The truth of Isaiah 55:11 is as astounding as it is mysterious. While we can't know all God's purposes, we do know that every purpose He ordains for the proclamation of His Word will succeed.

If you are a follower of Jesus, think about your testimony. How did you come to know the Lord? At some point, you encountered God's Word for the first time—searching it by yourself, hearing a pastor's sermon, listening to a friend share his faith, or even reading a book like this. However God's Word came to you, it did not return void. It's accomplishing everything God ordained in your life.

If that isn't cause for Christian joy and reflection—and a powerful motivation for evangelism—nothing is.

What can I do, right here, right now, to spread the unstoppable Word of God and watch Him work?

AGREEMENT VS. FAITH

You believe that there is one God. You do well;
the demons also believe, and tremble.

JAMES 2:19

✚

Nearly 90 percent of American adults believe in God or some sort of "higher power," according to a 2023 study conducted by the Pew Research Center. Of those individuals, 54 percent believe in "God as described in the Bible."

But are all those people true born-again Christians? In Matthew 7:14, Jesus said, "The gate is narrow and the way is narrow that leads to life, and there are few who find it." That doesn't sound like 90 percent.

Likewise, James 2:19 drives home the point: Simple mental assent that "Yes, there's a God" isn't enough. Even demons admit that.

Acknowledgment of God is a start, but He requires a living, active faith in His Son, Jesus, who made reconciliation with God possible through His death and resurrection. Don't just agree there's a God. Trust in His Son and follow Him in faith.

What can I do, right here, right now, to ensure that my knowledge of God is a true, living faith?

MORE IS BETTER

Pray without ceasing.
1 Thessalonians 5:17

In 1986, a man named Robert McDonald of Mariposa, California, set a Guinness World Record by staying awake for eighteen days, twenty-one hours, and forty minutes.

Yaaaawn.

So is this what scripture has in mind when it tells us to "pray without ceasing"? Does God want us to abstain from sleeping—as well as from eating, working, spending time with our family, and all our other daily activities—so we can pray all day, every day?

Of course not. This verse is simply an exhortation to make prayer a frequent part of our lives. Like Daniel (Daniel 6:10) and Nehemiah (see page 91), we should pray regularly each day. We can pray in good times and bad; at home, work, and church; while we're on the road and in bed.

The point is, pray without ceasing!

**What can I do, right here, right now,
to pray throughout the day?**

GET AFTER IT!

How long will you sleep, O sluggard?
When will you arise from your sleep?
PROVERBS 6:9

"The most active thing about me is my imagination."

"I've reached the pinnacle of laziness and gluttony. . . . How depressing. There's no place to go after you've reached the top."

"Would you be willing to lead a parade in celebration of the lazy life? If the answer is yes. . . you're all wrong for lazy week."

These quotes about laziness are from our favorite furry paragon of idleness, Garfield the cat. We laugh at Garfield's languid attitude, but truthfully, laziness is neither desirable nor godly. God created us to work. Even before the fall, work was part of God's perfect creation (Genesis 2:15).

Of course, rest and relaxation are necessary. Even God ceased His labors (Genesis 2:2). But we were never meant to be slothful in repose.

Work "heartily, as to the Lord," and you will be rewarded (Colossians 3:23–24).

What can I do, right here, right now, to fulfill the tasks God has given me?

A GOOD START

The statutes of the LORD are right,
rejoicing the heart. The commandment of the
LORD is pure, enlightening the eyes.

PSALM 19:8

✠

So often we tie ourselves in knots trying to determine God's will for our lives. We want Him to tell us exactly what to do in every important decision—school, work, home, marriage, kids, family drama, finances…and whether to buy an electric compact car that gets 984 miles per gallon (give or take) or a gas-guzzling cop magnet with a supercharged V-8. When we don't get a clear sign from heaven, we blame God.

Perhaps we should take our foot off the gas and read the Owner's manual.

God only holds us accountable for what He has revealed to us (Deuteronomy 29:29), and the Bible represents the perfect totality of God's revealed will. Does God's will feel hidden to you? Start by meditating on His "enlightening" Word.

What scripture addresses, obey. What it doesn't (like deciding between a Prius and a Mustang Shelby GT500), use wisdom and godly counsel.

Whatever you decide there, remember the speed limit.

**What can I do, right here, right now,
to seek God's will through scripture?**

A CHRISTIAN'S CALLING CARD

"By this shall all men know that you are My disciples, if you have love for one another."

JOHN 13:35

Some of the greatest criminal characters in cinematic history had unique calling cards—something they'd leave behind at the crime scene to hint at their identity. In *The Dark Knight*, Heath Ledger's sinister Joker left behind a joker playing card. In *Home Alone*, the inimitable Wet Bandits turned on all the water faucets in the house after their burglary was complete.

Of course, we're not encouraging you to dabble in criminal activity. But we as Christians have a calling card of our own: love.

For believers, genuine, godly love should be how we announce ourselves and what we leave with others. This is especially true in church. Jesus said in John 13:35 that "all men" will know we are His disciples "if you have love for one another."

May the calling card of Christlike love fill our churches and spill out the doors into a world that desperately needs it.

What can I do, right here, right now, to love my fellow believers?

UNITED JOY

*Fulfill my joy, that you be like-minded, having the
same love, being of one accord, of one mind.*

PHILIPPIANS 2:2

God wants us to be joyful. That's quite evident in scripture,
where some form of the word *joy* is used hundreds of times.
And while our individual salvation is the cause for continual
rejoicing, Christian joy is never meant to be experienced
in a vacuum. It's meant to be shared with other believers
in the regular gathering of God's people.

But church can get messy. After all, what is a local
church if not a group of redeemed sinners!

That's why Christian unity is essential. This is a con-
stant theme in scripture—from King David, who wrote,
"Behold, how good and how pleasant it is for brothers
to dwell together in unity!" (Psalm 133:1) to the apostle
Paul, who calls us to be "like-minded" and "of one accord"
(Philippians 2:2).

So seek unity. Forgive and seek forgiveness. Choose
humility over pride, and selflessness over selfishness.

Christian unity produces Christian joy.

**What can I do, right here, right now, to be
unified with my brothers and sisters in Christ?**

OVERCOMING THE WORLD

*"I have spoken these things to you, that in Me you might
have peace. In the world you shall have tribulation,
but be of good cheer: I have overcome the world."*

JOHN 16:33

The disciples had no idea what they were in for.

As Jesus spoke to His closest followers shortly before
His arrest, He told them they would experience incredible
persecution and trials. Indeed, according to scripture and
early church tradition, most—if not all—of Jesus' original
disciples (minus Judas Iscariot) suffered martyrdom.

But human pain and suffering, even death, do not
have the final word. Thanks to His atoning sacrifice and
glorious resurrection, Jesus does!

Our Lord has overcome sin and death. Jesus has overcome Satan and all the forces of evil. Jesus has overcome the
world and its anti-God machinations. Jesus has overcome
the power of sinful human flesh. Jesus has overcome every
trial you are going through.

Take heart, friend. Whatever you're enduring right
now, Jesus has ultimately defeated it, and through faith,
you will share in His eternal victory.

**What can I do, right here,
right now, to trust in Jesus' victory?**

TRUE REST

*"Come to Me, all you who labor and are
heavy-laden, and I will give you rest."*

MATTHEW 11:28

Rest is hard to come by these days. More than ever, it seems like our calendars are fuller, our workloads deeper, and our stress is higher. We all want a consistent good night's sleep, a healthy work/life balance, and the time and space to just. . .*be*. But how?

To every world-weary traveler of life, Jesus holds out a gentle, nail-scarred hand and offers rest. This isn't spiritual melatonin. Jesus offers rest for our minds, bodies, and souls. Because He has taken care of sin, our greatest problem, He offers the peace, joy, and hope that cannot be found anywhere else.

The calendar might still be full and the pile of papers on your desk high. But you can find true, abiding rest—spiritually, emotionally, mentally, and physically—in the Savior who makes us right with God.

**What can I do, right here,
right now, to rest in Christ?**

THE WORD OF GOD

*And He was clothed with a garment dipped in
blood, and His name is called The Word of God.*

REVELATION 19:13

✚

We often call the Bible "the Word of God." But to begin
his gospel, the apostle John referred to Jesus as "the Word"
of God (John 1:1). John did so again in Revelation 19:13.
So which is it? Is the Bible or Jesus the Word of God?

They both are!

Jesus, of course, is distinct from scripture. He is
supremely above all, and scripture magnifies Him, not
vice versa.

But John's play on words in these two passages was
no accident. Divinely inspired, John saw the relationship
between Jesus and scripture and masterfully connected
the two.

Jesus and scripture—both the living Word of God—are
sent from the Father. They reveal the Father and speak His
words to humanity. They communicate the Father's deep,
abiding love for His children. They glorify the Father. They
give us all we need for repentance, faith, and salvation.

**What can I do, right here, right now,
to exalt Jesus and treasure scripture?**

THE TRUE POWER OF FAITH

*That your faith should stand not in the
wisdom of men but in the power of God.*

1 CORINTHIANS 2:5

The ancient Greeks loved a good speech.

Rhetoric was a highly prized skill, and the Greeks devoted entire schools to teaching the art of persuasion through the spoken and written word. We see a glimpse of this in Acts 17, when Paul addressed the philosophers of the Areopagus on Mars Hill in Athens.

So when Paul wrote to the fledgling church in Corinth, a former Greek city-state in the Roman Empire, he encouraged his readers to put their faith in the God of scripture, not in a finely crafted oratory. "My speech and my preaching were not with enticing words of man's wisdom but in demonstration of the Spirit and of power," he wrote in 1 Corinthians 2:4.

Is your faith tied to persuasiveness of a human source? Or does it originate and draw its life from the power of God and the saving work of His Son, Jesus Christ?

What can I do, right here, right now, to trust in God's power rather than in human wisdom?

THE ANXIETY REMOVAL PLAN

Cast your burden on the LORD, and He shall sustain you; He shall never allow the righteous to be moved.

PSALM 55:22

✙

What makes you anxious? An impromptu meeting with your boss? A trip to the doctor's office? Certain social situations? Heights? Sharks? Clowns? A weekend with your in-laws?

Whatever it is, we all experience anxiety. It's that feeling of uneasiness, worry, or downright fear we get when difficulties arise—or threaten to. But scripture offers an amazing remedy for anxiety: prayer.

Prayer is a way to give our concerns to the God who cares for us (1 Peter 5:7). It's a humble admission that God can do things we can't. It's a faith-filled acknowledgement that He rules over all details, big and small, in life.

When you're anxious—about the stock market, your children's future, or spending time with the ol' mother-in-law—cast your burden on the Lord. Then, as Philippians 4:7 says, "the peace of God, which passes all understanding, shall guard your hearts and minds through Christ Jesus."

What can I do, right here, right now, to cast my burdens on God?

THIS MEANS WAR

Abstain from fleshly lusts that war against the soul.

1 PETER 2:11

The "Reconquista"—fought between the eighth and the fifteenth centuries in Europe—is generally considered the longest war in history. For a staggering 781 years, Spain and Portugal battled Moorish forces for control of the Iberian Peninsula. (Incidentally, this makes the Reconquista only slightly longer than the time required to play the card game "War" with your kids.)

As Christians, we too are locked in a heated, lifelong conflict: the war against our flesh. The sinful desires of our "old self" are a powerful, unrelenting foe. But the disciplined warrior of God doesn't give up, constantly engaging in battle through prayer, scripture, Christian fellowship, and the Spirit's power.

Best of all, in this protracted combat we have the ultimate weapon: the blood of Jesus, which vanquished the power of sin and death on the cross. "Those who are Christ's have crucified the flesh with the affections and lusts" (Galatians 5:24). We are victors through Jesus!

What can I do, right here, right now, to win the war against my sinful flesh?

GIFTED AND EQUIPPED

*Having then differing gifts according
to the grace that is given to us.*
ROMANS 12:6

✚

We've all heard the stories of the kid who *ooh'ed* and *aah'ed* at Major League Baseball players as a little ankle-biter—and then eventually became one. Others of us watched those same athletes on TV. . .and became sportswriters.

No matter what you do, your job doesn't define you. Your purpose in life goes far beyond your nine-to-five.

If you're a believer, God chose you for a specific purpose before time began (Ephesians 2), and He has intentionally hardwired you for success—according to *His* definition of success. To accomplish God's purpose, He has given you "spiritual gifts" (1 Corinthians 12:1), the special talents and leanings all believers have for building His kingdom. Descriptions of spiritual gifts (although not exhaustive) can be found in Romans 12:1–8, 1 Corinthians 12–14, and Ephesians 4:1–16.

So think about your wiring. What skills, abilities, and interests has God put in your heart? Through His Spirit, He has gifted and equipped you for success.

**What can I do, right here, right now,
to discover and employ my spiritual gifts?**

COUNTRY CLUB MEMBERSHIP: DENIED

As every man has received the gift, even so
minister the same to one another, as good
stewards of the manifold grace of God.

1 PETER 4:10

What comes to mind when you think of a country club?

A place to socialize and rub shoulders with like-minded, well-heeled individuals? A place to be waited upon? A place to casually chitchat about the wife, the kids, and the upcoming beach vacation, or to crow a bit about that new promotion? A comfortable place where you can forget about the world's problems for a while?

Now what comes to mind when you think of church?

God's church isn't a country club. It's not a place to be served, but to serve (Mark 10:45). It's a place to worship. It's a place to be challenged, encouraged, and equipped to advance God's kingdom.

When we enter church each week, let's enter with a Christlike attitude of humble servanthood. Let's use our gifts to minister to others. Let's ask ourselves, *What can I do for others today?*

What can I do, right here, right now,
to avoid a country-club mentality at church?

JOYFUL SERVICE

Serve the LORD with gladness;
come before His presence with singing.

PSALM 100:2

Scripture continually exhorts us to serve the Lord with joy. This isn't a fake happiness adorned with a plastic smile. God wants us to serve Him with true contentment and delight. In fact, in Deuteronomy 28:47–48, He warned Israel of judgment if they didn't.

Sounds harsh at first, but it's really not. God wants our hearts far more than our acts of piety. Grumbling service is not real obedience.

This is where our own self-centeredness and selfish ambition can clash with God's desires. Often, we are willing to serve God...in our own way and time. Yet isn't "convenient serving" an oxymoron?

As we gain a fuller understanding of who God is, what He's done for us in Christ, and why He created us, our joy in serving Him will grow. It will feel less like a duty (which it never was in the first place) and more like a great privilege.

What can I do, right here, right now,
to serve God with a joyful heart?

STRENGTH IN COMMUNITY

*Two are better than one, because they have a good
reward for their labor. For if they fall, the one will lift
up his companion, but woe to him who is alone when
he falls, for he does not have another to help him up.*

ECCLESIASTES 4:9–10

The Bible warns against Lone Ranger Christianity. It's not
only dangerous (it leaves us wide open to attack from the
evil one), but we are designed to work best in community.
Knowing we are part of a collective group with shared
values is far better than walking alone.

The hardships you experience are not unique. Countless
believers have endured similar trials—and often far worse—
yet remained faithful.

As you walk a hard path, remember that you're forever
linked through faith with other precious saints on the same
difficult journey. And you're all led by Jesus, "the author
and finisher of our faith" (Hebrews 12:2), who endured
the greatest trial of all for you.

**What can I do, right here, right now,
to be sure I'm not a Lone Ranger Christian?**

REAL ID

His head and His hair were white like wool,
as white as snow, and His eyes were like a flame of
fire. And His feet like fine brass, as if they burned in a
furnace, and His voice like the sound of many waters.

REVELATION 1:14–15

✛

Jesus' true identity has always puzzled many. Just as there were plenty of misunderstandings in the first century (Matthew 16:14), so there are today: powerful prophet, moralistic teacher, revolutionary leader, tragic martyr...the list goes on. Even many who profess Christianity see Him as nothing more than a long-haired life coach.

Then we come to the apostle John's encounter with Jesus in Revelation 1, and all our trifling preconceptions are blown to smithereens. The glory of the risen Savior was so overwhelming that it knocked John to the ground (Revelation 1:17), just as it had done to Paul years earlier (Acts 9:3–4).

Jesus is the Lord of heaven and earth, reigning on high. He holds the entire universe together (Colossians 1:17), and He will vanquish all evil with simply a word when He returns (Revelation 19:15). He is truly fearsome and awe-inspiring.

We would do well to worship Him as such.

**What can I do, right here, right now,
to better understand Jesus' true nature?**

A RESOUNDING *YES!*

For all the promises of God in Him are yes,
and in Him Amen, to the glory of God through us.

2 CORINTHIANS 1:20

If you've ever been around toddlers, you know what their favorite word is: *NO!*

Parents certainly don't teach this word to their kids. Neither do grandparents, family friends, or children's ministry workers at church. (Though maybe that cheeky Uncle Evan's been stirring up trouble.)

As fallen human beings, these adorable little bundles of joy instinctually know this word. And they use it. . .a lot.

Aren't you glad, then, for the truth of 2 Corinthians 1:20? The word *no* is nowhere to be found in this beautiful verse. All God's promises find a resounding *yes!* in Jesus.

Every promise of salvation, peace, joy, and future hope for believers in scripture—Old and New Testaments—has been fulfilled through Christ's perfect life, atoning death, and glorious resurrection. As Jesus Himself said, "I have come not to destroy but to fulfill" (Matthew 5:17).

Is this good news? Yes!

What can I do, right here,
right now, to say yes to Jesus?

FAITH + LOVE

*Though I have the gift of prophecy and understand
all mysteries and all knowledge, and though I
have all faith so that I could remove mountains,
and have not love, I am nothing.*

1 Corinthians 13:2

✦

Jesus said that even a small amount of faith—trusting in God's goodness and power—can accomplish great deeds. Mustard-seed faith can move mountains. But even mountain-moving faith is worthless without love.

God requires faith from His children, but love isn't just a nice optional add-on. It's an essential part of Christian faith. Genuine faith produces self-sacrificial love. To believe in the invisible God who visibly revealed His love to us in Christ is to show tangible, visible love to those around us.

When Jesus said, "Follow Me" (Matthew 4:19; 8:22; 9:9; 16:24; 19:21), He wasn't simply referring to the faith needed for salvation. He was calling us to a life of obedience, doing what He does, giving up ourselves for the good of others (Philippians 2:3–8).

Following Jesus involves faith *and* love.

**What can I do, right here, right now,
to supplement my faith with love for others?**

THE HARDEST PRAYER

"You have heard that it has been said,
'You shall love your neighbor and hate your enemy.'
But I say to you, love your enemies, bless those who
curse you, do good to those who hate you, and pray for
those who despitefully use you and persecute you."
MATTHEW 5:43–44

The Jewish religious leaders of Jesus' day had done a terrible job of interpreting the Old Testament scriptures. Jesus corrected one of these damaging misinterpretations in Matthew 5:43–44.

Somehow, the religious leaders had read about God's hatred toward sin and judgment of the wicked and concluded that pious Jews were allowed to hate their enemies. Jesus denounced this mindset and instead commanded us to "pray for those who. . .persecute you."

This is not an easy command. But Jesus expects it to be part of our prayer life. When we pray for our enemies, forgiveness and compassion will grow in our hearts, and God's love will be on display. Isn't that the goal?

What can I do, right here, right now, to develop
a heart for that person who mistreats me?

BE AN INFLUENCER

Do not be deceived:
"Evil company corrupts good manners."
1 CORINTHIANS 15:33

✚

In Disney's adaptation of the classic tale of Pinocchio, the wooden marionette who wants to become a real boy befriends a troublemaker named Lampwick, who nearly leads Pinocchio to ruin on Pleasure Island. It's an animated depiction of a timeless biblical truth: "Evil company corrupts good manners."

As we seek to be disciplined followers of Christ, it's important to surround ourselves with godly influences. Just as ink inevitably darkens a glass of water, so we cannot immerse ourselves in ungodly circles and come away unchanged.

From the beginning, God has called His children to be holy and set apart from unbelievers (Leviticus 20:26). This doesn't mean we are to be mountain-dwelling hermits. Rather, we are to live as children of light in a dark world. The friends and influences we allow into our lives are critical components of our spiritual walk—and our witness to a world that desperately needs Christ.

What can I do, right here, right now, to shift from ungodly to godly influences in my life?

DISCIPLES
MAKING DISCIPLES

*"Go and teach all nations, baptizing them in
the name of the Father and of the Son and of
the Holy Spirit, teaching them to observe all
the things that I have commanded you."*

MATTHEW 28:19–20

When it comes to finding and following our purpose as Christians, the Great Commission in Matthew 28:19–20 is like one of those free spaces in bingo. No matter what else happens, that space is a glorious gimme!

If you're a Christian, no matter who you are, where you live, what you do for a living, or what kind of personality you have, evangelism is a gimme. Jesus calls *all* His followers to be disciple-making disciples. This isn't only for Christians who are outspoken or good in front of crowds. This is God's will for every believer. And it's not a duty or a drudgery; it's an honor and a privilege.

Even if you're still working out the details of your purpose in life, remember your glorious gimme: You get to tell others about God's great love for them in Christ.

**What can I do, right here, right now,
to share my faith more actively with others?**

FEAR AND COMFORT
IN THE CHURCH

*Then the churches throughout all Judea and
Galilee and Samaria had rest and were edified.
And walking in the fear of the Lord and in the
comfort of the Holy Spirit, they were multiplied.*

ACTS 9:31

✛

The early Christian church had just endured a period of great persecution following Stephen's martyrdom as Saul ravaged the church. Then Saul miraculously turned to Jesus, became Paul the great missionary, and the churches enjoyed rest, peace, and multiplication.

But how? According to Acts 9:31, these things didn't come from fancy Sunday programming, a "relevant" youth group, or a top-notch coffee ministry. Rest, peace, and multiplication came as believers walked "in the fear of the Lord and in the comfort of the Holy Spirit."

Early Christians devoted themselves to gospel-soaked prayer and fellowship (Acts 2:42) and hands-on ministry (Acts 2:45)—the fear of the Lord. And they rejoiced that a better world awaited them through Christ—the comfort of the Holy Spirit. Let's do the same.

**What can I do, right here, right now,
to walk in the fear of the Lord and in
the comfort of the Holy Spirit?**

JOY AND PAIN

In the day of prosperity be joyful, but in the day of
adversity consider: God also has set the one alongside
the other, so that man would find nothing after him.

ECCLESIASTES 7:14

God is holy.
  God is love.
  God is gracious.
  God is merciful.
  God forgives our sins through Christ.

When we read these truths, our hearts are moved with thankfulness and praise toward God. But how do we respond when we read the following?

God has sovereignly ordained both joy and suffering.

That's a little harder to swallow. *How*, we wonder, *can God do this? Why would He allow this?* There is great mystery here, but scripture and our own experiences bear it out.

In His providential and often inscrutable wisdom, God has appointed both "the day of prosperity" and "the day of adversity." He works for our good in both (Romans 8:28). Trust Him. We won't experience true, lasting joy in life until we humbly acknowledge God's lordship in both and accept this by faith.

What can I do, right here, right now,
to remain joyful in adversity?

A MATTER OF UNDERSTANDING

Trust in the LORD with all your heart and do not lean on your own understanding. In all your ways acknowledge Him, and He shall direct your paths.

PROVERBS 3:5–6

Our society is built on learning. From an early age, we are taught our ABCs and 1-2-3s. Your academic performance in high school helps determine your college path. Many professions require a bachelor's degree, at minimum. Others require advanced degrees. Academic diplomas and extra learning can also bring promotions and pay raises.

We are wired to achieve through human wisdom. Yet God calls us to trust His wisdom, not ours. This is especially true in hardships when powerful emotions can cloud our judgment.

Are you walking a hard path now? Recognize your limitations and trust the Lord. Seek His perfect wisdom through prayer, His Word, and godly counsel. Lean on His power and love. Be sensitive to His Spirit.

As you do, He will guide you on a journey far better than one paved with your own understanding.

What can I do, right here, right now, to seek God's wisdom in trials?

RETURN OF THE KING

"Surely I come quickly."
REVELATION 22:20

✚

For those who love the Lord, there is no greater promise in scripture than these four words. Jesus is coming again—and "quickly"!

But wait, you say, *it's been two thousand years since He spoke those words! How is that quick?* Remember, friend, that "one day with the Lord is as a thousand years, and a thousand years as one day" (2 Peter 3:8). The eternal God—who sees past, present, and future simultaneously—keeps time a wee bit differently than we do.

At the proper time in history, God sent His Son to save us from our sins (Galatians 4:4–5). And at His appointed time in the future, God will send His Son once more to destroy all evil, renew His creation, and redeem His children.

One day, we'll be with our Savior forever, perfectly transformed into His image. So we wait with patience—and great anticipation.

Yes, Jesus is coming again. And to that we say, "Amen. Come, Lord Jesus!"

**What can I do, right here, right now,
to prepare for Jesus' return?**

BOOK OF HOPE

*Whatever things were written formerly were
written for our learning, that through patience and
comfort from the scriptures we might have hope.*

ROMANS 15:4

During his world-changing ministry, the apostle Paul wrote about virtually everything possible in the Christian life: marriage, sex, money, church, justification, sanctification, glorification—and everything in between.

But among Paul's favorite topics was hope. He mentioned it dozens of times in his letters, wanting Christians to be filled with "hope in our Lord Jesus Christ" (1 Thessalonians 1:3). He knew that the best place to find hope is in scripture.

The Bible is a book of hope. It lifts our eyes above the mundanities, pleasures, and trials of life and sets them on a future glory beyond our wildest imaginations. The Bible exhorts us to be "rejoicing in hope, patient in tribulation, continuing persistently in prayer" (Romans 12:12). Its truths cause us to lean forward with anticipation, "looking for that blessed hope and the glorious appearing of the great God and our Savior Jesus Christ" (Titus 2:13).

Need hope today? Open God's Word.

**What can I do, right here,
right now, to find hope in Christ?**

HOW FAITH SHIELDS US

*Above all, [take] the shield of faith, with which you
shall be able to quench all the fiery darts of the wicked.*

EPHESIANS 6:16

✚

The shield of faith is a prominent part of "the whole
armor of God" that Paul, in Ephesians 6, encourages every
Christian to put on in our daily spiritual battles. With the
shield of faith, we are able to "quench all the fiery darts of
the wicked." But how, exactly, does faith do this?

Faith is defensive armament against spiritual attacks.
Satan seeks to destroy with lies, accusations, deception,
and doubt. Faith guards against these things. Faith believes
God is loving, trustworthy, and powerful. Faith accepts
biblical truth in the midst of temptations and trials. Faith
remembers who we are now in Christ, not who we used
to be before Him.

When Satan's flaming arrows are hurtling toward
you, raise the shield of faith, fully trusting in our great,
loving God.

**What can I do, right here, right now, to let faith
be a protective shield for me in spiritual warfare?**

TRUE CONFESSIONS

*If we confess our sins, He is faithful and just to forgive
us our sins and to cleanse us from all unrighteousness.*

1 JOHN 1:9

✚

My bad.
> *Oops, sorry about that.*
> *I'll do better next time.*

How many times have people said these things to you?
How many times have you said them to others?

These phrases aren't very satisfying to hear when you've
been wronged. They don't sound like genuine repentance.
Sadly, we treat our own repentance like this too often.

We need to take confession of our sin seriously. This
takes place in prayer, and we're not fooling God when we
treat it flippantly. Thankfully, God is abundantly patient.
He promises full pardon when we prayerfully confess and
repent.

Jesus has already paid the price for our sins on the
cross, but sin still hurts our fellowship with God. May
we be quick to confess to the God who loves to forgive.

**What can I do, right here, right now, to make
confession a regular part of my prayers?**

DEATH IN THE FLESH,
LIFE IN THE SPIRIT

*If you live according to the flesh, you shall
die, but if through the Spirit you put to death
the deeds of the body, you shall live.*

ROMANS 8:13

The Roman Empire was awash in depravity. Drunkenness
and sexual immorality of all kinds were rampant, even
incorporated into pagan religious festivals. That's why
the New Testament writers spent so much time urging
first-century Christians—largely former pagans who once
practiced such debauchery—to leave their old ways behind.

Times haven't changed that much. Today's world is still
filled with the same kinds of lusts and evils. So we must
be on our guard. As Paul says in Romans 8:13, following
our own sinful passions is spiritual death. It's a dead-end
road that only leads to destruction (1 Corinthians 6:9–10).

Remember, if you're a believer, you have been spiritually reborn and newly "created according to God in
righteousness and true holiness" (Ephesians 4:24). So
choose to be different. Choose to be disciplined. Choose
to honor the Lord.

**What can I do, right here, right now,
to be spiritually disciplined with my body?**

KEEP ASKING

If any of you lacks wisdom, let him ask of God,
who gives to all men generously and without
reproach, and it shall be given him.

JAMES 1:5

It seemed so easy for David.

When he wondered whether he should attack the Philistines at Keilah, he asked God, "Shall I?" God said yes and David prevailed (1 Samuel 23:1–5). When David wondered whether he should hunt down a band of Amalekite raiders, he asked God, "Shall I?" God said yes and David prevailed (1 Samuel 30:1–20). When David wondered whether he should attack the Philistines after he became king (2 Samuel 2:1). . .well, you get the idea.

Yet in the specific decisions we face in our lives, God's will often seems more elusive. Still, scripture exhorts us to ask (James 1:5). Could it be that God wants to build our faith?

God doesn't play games with us. He always acts according to His perfect providence. So keep asking for guidance, clarity, and wisdom. He promises to answer.

**What can I do, right here,
right now, to seek God's wisdom?**

FIRST LOVE

"Nevertheless I have something against you,
because you have left your first love."

REVELATION 2:4

The first-century church in Ephesus seemed to be a thriving fellowship of believers, evidenced by Paul's beautiful, heartfelt New Testament letter to them and by the accounts of his interactions with them in Acts.

But several decades later, when John wrote Revelation, the Ephesian church had stumbled. The believers there seemed doctrinally sound, and Jesus (through John) also commended them for their "works" and "labor" (Revelation 2:2). But their passion for Christ had grown cold. They were going through the motions.

What an important reminder for us! Our churches today are filled with seminary-approved leaders and robust statements of faith, and we know how to work and labor in midweek programs like nobody's business.

But do we love Jesus? Do we worship Him and follow Him? Do we pursue His likeness and long for His return? Do we serve and love like He did?

May we never leave our first love—the Lord Jesus Christ.

**What can I do, right here, right now, to make
sure love for Jesus guides my works and labor?**

JOYFUL RECEPTION

"There are those [seeds] that were sown on stony ground, who, when they have heard the word, immediately receive it with gladness, and have no root in themselves, and so endure but for a time."

MARK 4:16–17

In the parable of the sower in Mark 4, Jesus uses a metaphor to illustrate four different human responses to hearing God's Word: There are those who allow Satan to snatch the Word from their hearts; there are those who initially receive the Word with joy but fall away in hardships; there are those who let the cares and pleasures of this world choke out the Word's truth; and there are those who receive the Word by faith and bear much spiritual fruit.

Which of these describes you?

Strive to retain the initial gladness you felt when you first encountered God's Word. Pray often to receive the life-changing truths of scripture with great joy—both now and in the future. May our joy in God's Word be as steadfast as scripture itself.

What can I do, right here, right now, to continue to receive God's Word with joy?

REJOICE. . .ALWAYS?

Rejoice always. Pray without ceasing.
Give thanks in everything, for this is the will
of God in Christ Jesus concerning you.
1 Thessalonians 5:16–18

Rejoicing is easy when your team wins the Super Bowl. Or when your kid gets into Harvard. Or when you hit the lottery.

Rejoicing is a lot harder, though, when a loved one dies. Or when your marriage ends. Or when your health screening reveals the dreaded *C*-word.

Yet scripture repeatedly tells us to be joyful in good times and bad. In fact, 1 Thessalonians 5:16 puts it like this: "Rejoice always."

The Bible isn't promoting fakeness, deceit, or hypocrisy. It's helping us drill down deeper—past the pain and suffering—into the spiritual well of God's goodness that never runs dry.

We don't rejoice in the pain itself. We rejoice in the God who walks beside us in it. This takes continual prayer (verse 17) and a stubbornly thankful heart (verse 18). It's not easy, but it's worth it.

**What can I do, right here, right now,
to position myself to rejoice always?**

FROM DEATH TO LIFE

But after that the kindness and love of God our Savior
toward man appeared, not by works of righteousness
that we have done, but according to His mercy
He saved us, by the washing of regeneration and
renewing of the Holy Spirit, whom He poured out
on us abundantly through Jesus Christ our Savior.

TITUS 3:4–6

Being dead stinks.

When you're dead, you can't do anything for yourself. You can't play racquetball, mow the lawn, or even watch *Gladiator* for the thirtieth time. You can't do anything because. . .well, you're dead.

Spiritually speaking, this is the terrible quandary we're all in from the moment we're born. Because of our sin nature, we start life "dead in trespasses and sins" (Ephesians 2:1). Our hearts are spiritually dead, incapable of self-correcting.

Thank God for the work of His Spirit! The Holy Spirit is God's agent of regeneration, softening hard hearts and transforming them to new life through faith in Jesus (1 Corinthians 15:22).

Sin brings death, but the Spirit brings life!

**What can I do, right here, right now,
to walk in the new life I have in Christ?**

LIFE-GIVING FOOD

"Man shall not live by bread alone, but by every word that proceeds out of the mouth of God."

MATTHEW 4:4

There's nothing like good bread. A hot, buttered cinnamon bagel in the morning? A juicy burger on a golden brown brioche bun? A pasta dish with warm, Italian seasoned breadsticks on the side? Yes, please!

But as delicious as good bread is, the human body needs more to survive. Jesus made this point during His temptation in the wilderness. But as He so often did, He turned everyday realities into powerful spiritual truth.

Just as food gives life to the physical body, God's Word gives life to our souls. If we don't regularly eat, we'll encounter all types of health problems. Likewise, if we don't regularly feed ourselves with scripture, we'll shrivel up and die spiritually.

The more you nourish yourself with biblical truth, the healthier you'll be as a follower of Christ. So dig in! God's Word supplies us with a never-ending heavenly feast.

What can I do, right here, right now, to nourish myself with life-giving scripture?

THE OPPOSITE OF DOUBT

*Immediately Jesus stretched out His hand and caught him,
and said to him, "O you of little faith, why did you doubt?"*
MATTHEW 14:31

✦

When Peter saw Jesus miraculously walking on the stormy
Sea of Galilee and stepped out of the boat toward his
Savior, he showed incredible faith. But when Peter turned
his attention from Jesus to the tempest swirling around
him, he began to sink and cried out for help. When Peter
trusted in Jesus' power, he did something remarkable. When
he doubted, he sank.

How true of our lives as well. Faith is the opposite of
doubt. When we trust in Jesus' perfect love, goodness, and
power, He will do remarkable things in us and through
us. But when we focus on the swirling tempest instead,
our doubts will cause us to sink into anxiety and despair.

Trust in Jesus. The same Savior who bid Peter, "Come"
on the stormy waters is reaching out His hand to you as well.

**What can I do, right here, right now,
to walk toward Jesus in faith?**

IF JESUS DID IT. . .

But the news about Him spread out even more,
and great multitudes came together to hear and
to be healed of their infirmities by Him. And He
withdrew Himself into the wilderness and prayed.

LUKE 5:15–16

We can so easily convince ourselves not to pray. *I don't really know how. I'm too busy. It's hard for me to sit still and focus. I'm not sure it really works anyway.* Then we read a passage like Luke 5:15–16, and all our feeble excuses not to pray are exposed.

Jesus prayed. Yes, the eternal Son of God, who created the universe and holds it together (Hebrews 1:2–3), prayed often while He was on earth. He withdrew to quiet, solitary places to speak to His heavenly Father. He prayed before His baptism (Luke 3:21), before choosing His disciples (Luke 6:12), and before His arrest and crucifixion (Matthew 26:39). He even prayed for you (John 17:20–21)!

In His humanity, Jesus needed prayer. And if that was the case for God's incarnated Son, then how much more is it true for us?

What can I do, right here,
right now, to pray like Jesus?

THE BEAUTY OF SELF-DENIAL

"If any man wants to come after Me, let him
deny himself, and take up his cross, and follow Me.
For whoever will save his life shall lose it, and
whoever will lose his life for My sake shall find it."

MATTHEW 16:24–25

✢

The disciples were confused.

They thought Jesus had come to earth to free them
from Roman oppression and inaugurate an earthly kingdom.
They expected to rule with Him and jockeyed for position
as they anticipated worldly prestige and power. Peter even
rebuked Jesus when Jesus spoke of His coming death. So
Jesus readjusted their thinking in Matthew 16:24–25.

Following Jesus isn't about amassing position, prestige,
and power in the here and now. It's about servanthood and
self-denial. It's about building an eternal kingdom.

Christian self-denial isn't meant to veer into asceti-
cism (see Colossians 2:16–23). Rather, the Christian life is
about denying our own sinful pride and selfish desires and
submitting to the lordship of Christ. In this self-denial,
there is great eternal gain.

**What can I do, right here, right now,
to deny myself and follow Jesus?**

ALIGNING OUR HEARTS

Delight yourself also in the LORD,
and He shall give you the desires of your heart.

PSALM 37:4

For a variety of reasons, as life progresses, many of us develop of warped view of God and His character. We come to think of God as some sort of divine miser, the scrooge of heaven who revels in withholding blessings from His children.

Nothing could be further from the truth!

God takes delight in *blessing* His children (Psalm 35:27). In fact, every good gift we enjoy comes from Him (James 1:17).

So when you need wisdom to understand and pursue God's will, ask for it. God delights to give you the desires of your heart. . .when the desires of your heart align with His. The more our hearts desire the Lord, the more He'll give us the desires of our hearts. That's a sweet deal.

**What can I do, right here, right now,
to delight myself in the Lord?**

GO, TELL!

"Repentance and remission of sins should be preached in His name among all nations."

LUKE 24:47

✚

When we leave home for an extended period, the last thing we say to our loved ones is usually important. Whether it's instructions during our absence or a simple "I love you," those parting words carry extra weight. It's what we want the listener to remember most while we're gone.

Shortly before He ascended into heaven, Jesus told His disciples to "go and teach all nations" about Him (Matthew 28:19). This Great Commission is the message He wants filling our hearts and motivating our actions until He returns.

Jesus wants His church to be full of faithful disciples who make other disciples. His message of "repentance and remission of sins" is to be "preached. . .among all nations" (Luke 24:47). But "how shall they believe in Him of whom they have not heard? And how shall they hear without a preacher?" (Romans 10:14).

So we must go, tell, and make disciples!

**What can I do, right here, right now,
to be a disciple-maker for Christ?**

MISPLACED JOY

*"Do you not know this of old, since man was placed
on earth, that the triumphing of the wicked is short,
and the joy of the hypocrite but for a moment?"*

Job 20:4–5

✝

Why do the wicked prosper while the righteous suffer?

It's a vexing question—one that has been asked since ancient times. Asaph asked it in Psalm 73. Solomon wrote about it in Ecclesiastes 7:15. David, Habakkuk, Jeremiah, Job, and other biblical figures all wondered the same thing.

Have you ever asked this in your heart? Have you ever wondered why you should take joy in pursuing righteousness when so many people seem perfectly happy, healthy, and content to pursue it elsewhere?

Scripture's answer is to take the long view. In this short life, evildoers might prosper, but with eternity in mind, "the triumphing of the wicked is short." Read Psalm 73:17 for more.

Don't fall prey to the vain, fleeting pursuit of worldly happiness. Find your joy and contentment forever in the Lord.

**What can I do, right here, right now, to
seek joy in God's righteousness?**

MINISTRY OF COMFORT

Blessed be God, even the Father of our Lord Jesus
Christ, the Father of mercies and the God of all comfort,
who comforts us in all our tribulation, that we may
be able to comfort those who are in any trouble, by the
comfort with which we ourselves are comforted by God.
2 CORINTHIANS 1:3–4

Many people have a warped view of God. Some see God
as distant and uncaring. Others see God as a miser or a
killjoy who prefers to take rather than give. Still others see
God as always angry.

Yet scripture says otherwise. Second Corinthians 1:3,
in particular, speaks of God as "the Father of mercies and
the God of all comfort." What's more, God invites us to be
a conduit of His mercy and comfort to others. Amazing!

Do you know someone who is suffering? Bring comfort to that person and show mercy. By doing so, you'll
be revealing the God of all comfort to someone who
desperately needs Him.

**What can I do, right here, right now,
to comfort someone in need?**

THE NEW TEMPLE OF GOD

*Do you not know that you are the temple of God
and that the Spirit of God dwells in you?*

1 Corinthians 3:16

For more than one thousand years, God met with His people in the special place of His presence—first the tabernacle, and then the temple. Even after King Nebuchadnezzar and the Babylonians sacked Jerusalem and destroyed the temple in 586 BC, the Jews rebuilt the temple and worshipped there for nearly six hundred more years until the Romans destroyed it for good in AD 70. The temple has never been rebuilt.

But that age has passed. Now, thanks to the new covenant purchased with Christ's blood, God again dwells in His temple—and His temple is *us*. God's Spirit now lives inside every true believer, filling us with His love, joy, power, peace, and hope.

The indwelling of the Spirit is as mysterious as it is marvelous. But if you are a Christ-follower, it's real and it's available to you now and forevermore.

**What can I do, right here,
right now, to tap into the Spirit of
God's presence living inside of me?**

COMPREHENSIVE COLLECTION

He said to me, "Write, for these words
are true and faithful."

REVELATION 21:5

✚

Think for a moment about all the books you've ever read. Have they all been one genre? No, of course not.

Aren't you glad that God is perfectly creative and that He packed His Word with purposeful variety? Scripture is filled with historical narratives, songs, poetry, proverbs, prophecies, letters, and visions of the future. He knows we like stories, so the Bible features true tales of kingdoms, empires, kings, queens, armies, heroes, villains, angels, demons, miracles, and much more. He knows we often learn best by learning about the triumphs and failures of others like us.

Sometimes He directly dictated the words of scripture to human authors. Other times He guided them quietly by His Spirit. All combined, the sixty-six books of the Bible tell one beautifully true and comprehensive story of God's redeeming love for lost humanity.

Happy reading!

**What can I do, right here, right now,
to savor the beautiful variety of the Bible?**

PUTTING SIGHT ASIDE

We walk by faith, not by sight.
2 CORINTHIANS 5:7

We are a sight-based people.

We learn with our eyes. We drive with our eyes. We work, play sports, and watch movies with our eyes. When our kids say, "No, really, my bedroom is clean," we, like Doubting Thomas, respond, "I'll believe it when I see it!"

But Christians are called to do something radical. God tells us to eschew sight and walk by faith. We must trust without seeing. We must believe in spiritual realities that human eyes cannot detect.

This is hard, but it's vital. We must believe there's a God we can't see, a crucified Savior who's now alive, a Spirit who lives inside us, and an eternal home awaiting for all who have faith.

Do we believe in God? Do we trust in Jesus? Do we hope in unseen promises? If we are to follow Christ, we must.

But soon, our faith will become sight. Then "we shall be like Him, for we shall see Him as He is" (1 John 3:2).

**What can I do, right here, right now,
to trust God more than my eyes?**

GROANINGS OF THE SPIRIT

Likewise the Spirit also helps our infirmities.
For we do not know what we should pray for as we
ought, but the Spirit Himself makes intercession
for us with groanings that cannot be uttered.

ROMANS 8:26

As humans, we love going behind the scenes. This is why we take backlot tours at Universal Studios, watch shows like *Access Hollywood*, and daydream about meeting our favorite musical artist with a backstage pass.

One of the great beauties—and mysteries—of the Christian life is what's happening behind the scenes in the spiritual realm, especially when we pray. Jesus, our great high priest, is at God's right hand, mediating for us (Romans 8:34). So is the Holy Spirit. In fact, when we don't know what to pray for, the Spirit takes up our cause, interceding with God on our behalf.

This is incredible! How does it all work? What do Jesus and the Spirit say in our stead? Much is shrouded in mystery. But take heart: The love and care—indeed, even the prayers—of heaven are behind you.

What can I do, right here,
right now, to grow in my prayer life?

THE GOD WHO LOVES TO GIVE

O taste and see that the LORD is good. Blessed is the man who trusts in Him. O fear the LORD, you His saints, for there is no lack for those who fear Him.

PSALM 34:8–9

In secular and Christian circles alike, there's a false narrative out there about following Jesus. Many people think Christianity is nothing more than a rigid lifestyle that restricts the enjoyment of life and promotes monkish self-denial.

Nothing could be further from the truth.

While followers of Christ are called to deny their sinful passions and pleasures, choosing godliness instead, this new way of living brings pure, lasting joy that can't be found anywhere else in this transient world. As Christians, we serve a God who lavishes His children with countless blessings. He supplies all our needs (Philippians 4:19) and so much more (Ephesians 3:20–21).

There's no end to the spiritual blessings God gives to those who follow Him. Taste and see that the Lord is good!

What can I do, right here, right now, to better trust in God's abundant goodness?

NO LONERS ALLOWED

The way of a fool is right in his own eyes,
but he who listens to counsel is wise.

PROVERBS 12:15

✚

Lone wolves might be great protagonists in Hollywood. But when we try to be John Wayne, Clint Eastwood, or Steve McQueen in real life, it typically doesn't work out too well.

God created us to live in community, not isolation. This includes the big decisions we face. Are you trying to determine your purpose? Are you seeking God's will in a difficult situation? Do you need to know which path to take at a crossroads? Don't walk alone. God never intended us to do so.

Wise counsel is a gift from God. In fact, it's often the way He guides us. The book of Proverbs is filled with exhortations to surround ourselves with godly advice. Wise believers can often see blind spots and offer perspectives we haven't considered.

When you're facing a tough choice, show some true grit and welcome the godly input of others.

What can I do, right here, right now,
to welcome the perspective of wise believers?

UNITED WE STAND

*Now I beseech you, brothers, by the name of our Lord Jesus
Christ, that you all speak the same thing and that there be
no divisions among you, but that you be perfectly joined
together in the same mind and in the same judgment.*

1 CORINTHIANS 1:10

The first-century church in Corinth was a hot mess.

Pride and division threatened to rip the church apart.
The Corinthian believers struggled with leadership factions,
lawsuits, arguments over pagan temple food, the flouting of
social pecking orders, and clamoring for "elite" spiritual gifts.

Paul appealed several times in writing for the church
to repent and embrace unity. Years after Paul's martyrdom,
as younger men boorishly worked to oust older men from
church leadership, first-century church leader Clement
fought the same battle.

What became of the Corinthian church? We don't
know. But for several decades at least, its witness was stunted
by pride, selfishness, divisions, and infighting.

These things have no place in the house of God. May
our churches be different. May *we* be different.

**What can I do, right here, right now,
to promote unity within my church?**

YET. . .REJOICE

Yet I will rejoice in the LORD.
I will rejoice in the God of my salvation.

HABAKKUK 3:18

The prophet Habakkuk was vexed.

Evil permeated the nation of Judah. And God was about to bring judgment through the Babylonians—a wicked nation that was even more godless than Judah.

Why are you allowing all this, God? This was Habakkuk's cry. We've all been there. Maybe you're there now.

God's answer, distilled to its simplest essence, is found in Habakkuk 2:4: "The just shall live by. . .faith."

As Habakkuk wondered, he also remembered. He recalled God's love, mercy, power, and faithfulness in the past. And his doubt turned to joy. "Although the fig tree shall not blossom. . .and there shall be no herd in the stalls, yet I will rejoice in the LORD" (Habakkuk 3:17–18).

When all seems lost and life looks hopeless, rejoice (like Habakkuk did) in the Lord and His salvation. He is just and true. He is worthy of your faith.

What can I do, right here, right now,
to rejoice in the midst of suffering?

ESCAPE KEY

No temptation has taken you but such as is
common to man. But God is faithful, who will
not allow you to be tempted above what you are
able, but with the temptation will also make a
way of escape, that you may be able to bear it.

1 CORINTHIANS 10:13

When we are in the crucible of life's trials, it can feel like we're trapped in an escape room. . .with no escape. Like the writer of Lamentations, we cry, "He has hedged me in so that I cannot get out. He has made my chain heavy. Also when I cry and shout, He shuts out my prayer" (3:7–8).

This is what intense suffering *feels* like. But God never abandons us, and He never gives us more than we can bear—as we continue to seek Him.

And there's the kicker. Many of life's trials *are* too much for us to bear—on our own. But by resting in the God whose peace, power, and wisdom are infinitely greater than ours, we can withstand any temptation, endure any trial, and find the escape key.

What can I do, right here, right now,
to cling to God in temptations and trials?

A WELCOME PRESENCE

*"And when He comes, He will convict the world
of sin and of righteousness and of judgment."*

JOHN 16:8

Prior to His death and resurrection, Jesus told His disciples that it was better for them that He would soon return to heaven. The disciples certainly must have been stunned. *How can it possibly be better for You to leave rather than stay with us?* they must have thought. Jesus' answer: Because His departure would pave the way for the Holy Spirit's arrival.

In the incarnation, the eternal Son of God willingly and temporarily accepted some of the limitations of finite humanity, such as only being able to be present in one place at one time. But the Holy Spirit continually lives in the hearts of all believers worldwide. The Spirit helps us discern God's will, determine right from wrong, and experience helpful conviction when we sin. Only with His continual presence in us can we please the Father and grow in Christ.

Praise God for His Spirit's convicting presence in our lives.

**What can I do, right here, right now, to be more
sensitive to the Spirit's conviction in my life?**

NAKED AND OPEN

There is no creature that is not made plain in His
sight, but all things are naked and opened to the
eyes of Him with whom we have to answer to.
HEBREWS 4:13

Open. Vulnerable. Chatty. Talkative. Caring. Sensitive.

Somewhere along the way, these words became slights
in the minds of the typical American male. *Vulnerability is
for suckers! Play it close. Play it cool. Play it like James Bond.*
Or so the thinking goes.

God sees straight through this. As Hebrews 4:12–13
says, His Word discerns "the thoughts and intentions of
the heart" and exposes us as "naked and opened" before
our Creator. So much for being 007.

But this is a good thing. To barricade our hearts and
remain aloof toward God is spiritual death. (And it doesn't
really work well in human relationships either.)

Strong and silent might work on the silver screen. But
in real life, less secret agent and more humble openness
will take you far.

**What can I do, right here, right now,
to let scripture reveal my true heart?**

PILGRIM'S PROGRESS

*These all died in faith, not having received the
promises, but having seen them from afar and were
persuaded of them, and embraced them, and confessed
that they were foreigners and pilgrims on the earth.*

HEBREWS 11:13

It's hard to read the "Hall of Faith" in Hebrews 11 and
not marvel at the remarkable faith described within. Yet as
Hebrews 11:13 says, all these Old Testament saints "died
in faith." They heard God's promises, and some of them
even witnessed partial fulfillment, but none lived to see
the full realization of God's plans. They understood they
were only "foreigners and pilgrims on the earth," awaiting
a better home.

We need the same mindset today. As followers of
Christ, we too must recognize that we are simply passing
through this earth as pilgrims, awaiting our forever home.
What propels us forward in this difficult, exilic lifestyle?

Faith.

We long for God's promises to be completely fulfilled
and expectantly await our Savior. So we hope in faith. And
this hope will not disappoint us (Romans 5:5).

**What can I do, right here, right now,
to embrace my pilgrim status on this earth?**

PERSISTENT PRAYER

Rejoicing in hope, patient in tribulation,
continuing persistently in prayer.
ROMANS 12:12

Romans 12:12 is one of those great verses of scripture that are succinct, memorable, provocative, and powerful. Stick it on a coffee mug. Slap it on a T-shirt. Tape it to your bathroom mirror. It's a mantra that every Christian should follow.

As followers of Jesus, we can rejoice in an abundance of hope through the finished work of Christ. Yet the tribulations we face in this fallen world can be excruciatingly hard. This calls for patient endurance.

Through it all, we must persist in prayer. Thank God for the good. Cry out to Him in the bad. Wrestle through doubts and fears with Him at your side. Praise Him in all things.

Prayer is our lifeline, our hiding place, our refuge when the tempests of life seem to be tearing down everything around us. So keep on praying, friend. Continue. Endure. Persevere. Persist. God will answer in His good time.

**What can I do, right here, right now,
to faithfully persist in prayer?**

BODY ISSUES

*Therefore I beseech you, brothers, by the mercies of God,
that you present your bodies as a living sacrifice, holy,
acceptable to God, which is your reasonable service.*

ROMANS 12:1

The human body is truly a remarkable thing. With it we can write stories, create music, play sports, build civilizations, cure diseases, and fly to the moon.

But too often, we—Christians and non-Christians alike—don't take care of the wonderful gift that God has given us in our bodies. We overeat. We don't exercise. We consume harmful outside substances that rot us from the inside out. We look at things that desecrate ourselves and others.

Our bodies are not meant to be cruise ships of worldly pleasure. They are divinely created temples of the living God, meant to be houses of worship and vessels of godly service.

So let's treat them as such. Let's present our bodies as a living sacrifice with all appropriate self-care and discipline—to honor the Lord and serve others.

What can I do, right here, right now, to better care for my body, the temple of the living God?

PLANNING AHEAD

There are many plans in a man's heart; nevertheless,
the counsel of the LORD—that shall stand.

PROVERBS 19:21

✚

Our lives today really aren't possible without planning. We
have calendars in our computers, phones, day planners. . .and
some of us still stick calendars to our refrigerators with
magnets! We plan sunup to sundown. We plan our home
lives, work lives, and upcoming vacations. We plan hair-
cuts, oil changes, trips to the supermarket, the kids' school
schedules, the timing of every ride at Disney, and our last
will and testaments.

Yet life often doesn't follow our plans. The car breaks
down. Job status changes. A spouse leaves. A loved one
gets cancer. Try as we might, we can't be certain about
the future. We can plan, but God's purposes will prevail.

The Bible never tells us not to plan. But it does tell
us to acknowledge that *God* is in control of everything.
So plan away. . .but remember that God rules over all,
including your calendar.

What can I do, right here, right now,
to submit my plans to God?

DEALING WITH CHURCH HURT

Be kind to one another, tenderhearted, forgiving one another, even as God for Christ's sake has forgiven you.

EPHESIANS 4:32

✚

There's no hurt like church hurt. When the place that is supposed to be filled with God's love causes intense grief, it can be spiritually discombobulating. The wounds can take years to heal.

God's church is made up of sinners, just like you. Redeemed sinners, to be sure, but sinners nonetheless. Remember, the failings of God's people reflect on us, not Him. He is holy, righteous, and loving. On our best days, we're but a dim reflection of His goodness.

So fight bitterness and seek to forgive, just as God through Christ has forgiven you for infinitely more wrongs. It might take a month. It might take years. But only through forgiveness will true healing come.

If you've never experienced church hurt before, be thankful. But also be aware and sensitive to those who have. It's real, and its victims need the loving, compassionate touch of Christ through you.

What can I do, right here, right now, to forgive fellow believers who have wronged me?

BIG-PICTURE JOY

"Well done, good and faithful servant. You have been
faithful over a few things; I will make you ruler over
many things. Enter into the joy of your lord."
MATTHEW 25:21

We often search for joy in brief, exciting experiences. The purchase of a new home. A weeklong trip to the Caribbean. A vacation at Disney (though some might say that brings the opposite of joy). A new job or a big promotion. A guys' weekend in the mountains. Sex with your wife. While these things can all be very good, the Bible challenges us to seek ultimate joy not in the gifts of the Master but in the Master Himself.

In Jesus' parable of the talents (Matthew 25), the faithful servants were invited to "enter into the joy" of their master (verses 21, 23). This joy didn't come from a short-lived experience but from consistent, faithful service over a long period.

Faithful Christian service leads to eternal spiritual joy.

What can I do, right here, right now, to serve
with joy—to experience even greater joy?

INCOMPARABLE

*For I consider that the sufferings of this present
time are not worthy to be compared with
the glory that shall be revealed in us.*

ROMANS 8:18

If anyone knew suffering, it was the apostle Paul.

Virtually from the moment he encountered the risen Savior on the road to Damascus, Paul's life became one harrowing event after another. In 2 Corinthians 11:23–29, he lists many of the hardships he endured, including hunger, thirst, beatings, whippings, a stoning, shipwrecks, imprisonments, and continual animosity from others.

Yet Paul was able to write the words of Romans 8:18 truthfully and with conviction.

Scripture has given us small glimpses of what eternity will look like for followers of Christ, but much of it remains to be seen. Yet we can rest assured that it will be glorious beyond our wildest imagination.

Believer, no matter what you're enduring right now, remember this: Our sufferings in this world will pale in comparison to our joys in the next!

**What can I do, right here, right now,
to look forward to the glory to come?**

SANCTIFICATION OF THE SPIRIT

But you were washed, but you were sanctified,
but you were justified in the name of the
Lord Jesus and by the Spirit of our God.

1 CORINTHIANS 6:11

Our spiritual growth is both a process and a partnership. The moment God justifies us through faith in Christ and we become believers, we start a journey of sanctification—becoming more like Jesus—that will culminate in eternally glorified bodies when Jesus returns.

But sanctification isn't magic. God doesn't wave a wand to—*poof!*—instantly sanctify us. Instead, it's a daily—and sometimes painful—process of growing in Christ through the transforming work of the Holy Spirit.

Yet even as God's Spirit works in us, we also have a responsibility. As we actively put off the "old self" of our sinful nature and put on the newness of Christ, we mature as believers. There will be setbacks along the way because of our sin, but by God's grace and the Spirit's help, we will slowly but surely move forward into Christlikeness.

**What can I do, right here, right now,
to grow in my sanctification?**

WISE FOR SALVATION

*From childhood you have known the holy
scriptures, which are able to make you wise for
salvation through faith that is in Christ Jesus.*
2 TIMOTHY 3:15

Timothy enjoyed a great spiritual head start in life. While his father was an unbelieving Greek (Acts 16:1, 3), his mother and grandmother were both believers (2 Timothy 1:5) who taught him scripture "from childhood," and Timothy came to saving faith in Christ.

Is that your story? Did you grow up in a family in which God's Word was cherished and taught? Or was your experience the opposite? Regardless, it is ultimately God's Word—not family upbringing—that makes us "wise for salvation through faith. . .in Christ Jesus."

Many books (including this devotional) can be helpful in your spiritual journey. But only the Bible is the inspired, inerrant, and sufficient Word of God that holds forth the very words of God for eternal life.

Just like Timothy did, run to it. Believe it. And live by it.

**What can I do, right here, right now,
to be wise for salvation through scripture?**

COMFORT FOR THE WEARY

*All things were created by Him
and for Him. And He is before all things,
and by Him all things consist.*

COLOSSIANS 1:16–17

✚

Scripture is abundantly clear: Jesus was not created. As the eternal Son of God and the second person of the Trinity, He has always existed and always will. As such, He is perfectly and exclusively qualified to be "the author and finisher of our faith" (Hebrews 12:2).

As part of the immortal Godhead, Jesus authored our faith by choosing us before the world began (Ephesians 1:4), making us right with God through His atoning death and resurrection (Colossians 1:19–20), and starting His church (Colossians 1:18). Likewise, He will finish our faith by completing our sanctification process and returning to bring us into heavenly glory (1 Thessalonians 5:23).

Can there be a greater comfort for weary Christian pilgrims? The faith Jesus started in us, He will perfectly complete.

**What can I do, right here, right now,
to trust more deeply in Jesus' eternal power
and care as He completes His work in me?**

JESUS' PRAYER FOR YOU

"I do not ask for these alone, but also for those who shall believe in Me through their word, that they all may be one, as You, Father, are in Me, and I in You, that they also may be one in Us, that the world may believe that You have sent Me."

JOHN 17:20–21

What a moment that must have been for Jesus' disciples to hear Him lift them up to God in the "High Priestly Prayer" of John 17. Yet incredibly, in that moment shortly before His arrest and crucifixion, Jesus also prayed for us!

Prior to entering the garden of Gethsemane that evening, Jesus prayed for the unity of His future followers. This is incredibly significant. Above all, Jesus prayed for believers to be united in His love, which would result in a powerful witness to a watching world.

Do you seek harmony with other believers? Do you pray for unity within your circles of Christian fellowship? This was—and is—Christ's prayer for you.

What can I do, right here, right now, to pray for and seek unity in the body of Christ?

LOVING THE LAW

I will delight myself in Your
commandments, which I have loved.

PSALM 119:47

Have you ever considered how extraordinary—and anti-thetical to our human way of thinking—Psalm 119 is? As prideful sinners, we were born with rebellious hearts toward God. We don't like being told what to do.

Yet in Psalm 119, the writer continually expresses his deep, abiding love for God's laws. Here are a few examples: "I will delight myself in Your statutes" (verse 16); "Behold, I have longed for Your precepts" (verse 40); "Your statutes have been my songs in the house of my pilgrimage" (verse 54); "The law of Your mouth is better to me than thousands of gold and silver" (verse 72); "O how I love Your law! It is my meditation all day" (verse 97).

Oh, that we would love God's laws like the psalmist! Oh, that we would prize His precepts! Oh, that we would cherish His Word!

What can I do, right here, right now,
to grow in my love for God's good laws?

UNDERSTANDABLE INSCRUTABILITY

O the depth of the riches both of the wisdom and knowledge of God! How unsearchable are His judgments and His ways past finding out!

ROMANS 11:33

✚

We are a curious—and sometimes skeptical—people. We often don't like what we don't understand.

Over the course of history, this quest for knowledge and understanding has led to amazing, history-shaping discoveries. But when it comes to spiritual matters, our desire to understand all things can lead to trouble (Genesis 3:5). God has revealed much to us in His Word. Yet much more about God's ways—and God Himself—is often inscrutable.

This shouldn't be hard to accept. After all, God is infinite, holy, and righteous—and we are not. Let's embrace the inscrutability of God. A god who can be fully known by limited, fickle humans isn't much of a god. But a God whose ways are far greater than ours? That's a God who is worthy of praise.

What can I do, right here, right now, to honor God for His inscrutable ways?

THE MINISTRY OF LOVE

Now remain faith, hope, love, these three.
But the greatest of these is love.

1 CORINTHIANS 13:13

Ah, good ol' 1 Corinthians 13—the Bible's "love chapter." Perhaps more than any other chapter in scripture, it is mined for engagement announcements and wedding sermons.

But Paul originally wrote this chapter in a completely different context—to encourage the Corinthian Christians to use their spiritual gifts *in love* toward one another. Paul's message was clear: God's church should be marked by love.

Pastors, elders, and deacons need to be marked by love. So do worship team members, ministry directors, and small group leaders. The same goes for children's ministry teachers, nursery workers, lobby greeters—and everyone who calls themselves a follower of Jesus.

Many of today's churches excel at technology, programming, and production value. But if all our efforts aren't marked by love, we become "as sounding brass or a tinkling cymbal" (1 Corinthians 13:1). Loveless deeds, as splendid as they can sometimes appear, profit us nothing (verse 3).

In everything you do, do it in love.

What can I do, right here, right now, to sacrifice myself for the good of others at church?

EMPTY TOMB, GREAT JOY

And they departed quickly from the sepulchre with fear
and great joy, and ran to bring His disciples word.
MATTHEW 28:8

✝

Have you ever "departed quickly from the sepulchre with fear and great joy"? Probably not. In our culture, we visit the graves of loved ones to pay our respects, to grieve a loss, and to remember. The trip back home is usually painful and somber.

Consider, then, the radically different experience that Mary Magdalene and the other women had when they departed Jesus' tomb on Resurrection Sunday. The tomb was empty! The Savior had risen! Jesus was alive!

Today, even though we aren't firsthand witnesses to the empty tomb, our joy should be just as great as that of those first-century believers. Why? Because Jesus' death and resurrection provides to us the same forgiveness of sins. It offers us the same peace and comfort. And it gives us the same hope of eternal life with Christ.

Today and always, praise God for the resurrection with "great joy."

**What can I do, right here, right now,
to rejoice in Christ's resurrection?**

NO SEPARATION ANXIETY

Who shall separate us from the love of Christ?
Shall tribulation, or distress, or persecution,
or famine, or nakedness, or peril, or sword?
ROMANS 8:35

When the Nazis began rounding up Jews throughout Europe at the outset of World War II, Adolf Hitler's abominable "Final Solution" separated countless Jewish families, sending millions to their deaths in his horrific extermination camps. But over the years, a number of heartwarming stories have surfaced of couples reuniting years—or even decades—later. It's hard to fathom the depths of despair these victims must have felt during their separation.

All true followers of Jesus have the great assurance that they will never be separated from Christ. Nothing, not even the worst hardships that life brings, can sever our spiritual union with Him.

If you have trusted in Jesus as your Lord and Savior, know that you're secure in His love. That's because your salvation is based solely and exclusively on His love and His atoning work on the cross. And nothing in this world can change that.

What can I do, right here, right now,
to better grasp the security of Christ's love?

FORGET-ME-NOTS

"The Comforter, who is the Holy Spirit,
whom the Father will send in My name,
He shall teach you all things and bring to your
remembrance all things that I have said to you."

JOHN 14:26

We all need reminders from time to time. Maybe it's the string tied around your finger or a prominently placed sticky note, or an electronic calendar chime. Whatever method you use, we all need prompts to remember important details each day.

The same is true in our spiritual lives. That's one of the main reasons God has given us His Spirit. As Jesus told His disciples, the Holy Spirit helps us remember Jesus' words and guides us into God's truth (John 16:13).

This is vitally important because whether it's remembering an anniversary, picking up a birthday gift, or recalling scripture in a moment of need, we are a forgetful lot. Thankfully, the Holy Spirit is ever-present in our lives to remind us of eternal truth.

What can I do, right here, right now,
to listen to the Holy Spirit's guidance?

WANTING TO BE KNOWN

By revelation He made known to me the
mystery (as I wrote before in few words,
by which, when you read it, you may understand
my knowledge of the mystery of Christ).

In the ancient world, pagans were constantly trying to figure out the will of the gods. They prayed, danced, fornicated, cut themselves, searched the stars, studied animal entrails, and even performed child sacrifices—all in an attempt to understand the gods and earn their favor.

Thankfully, the one true God of the Bible doesn't work like that. He *wants* to be known by us.

Of course, there is much mystery to God. He is infinite and we are not, by a long shot. But He isn't aloof. He has marvelously revealed Himself to us in many ways—through creation (Romans 1:19–20), His Spirit (1 Corinthians 2:9–10), our innate longing for spiritual matters (Ecclesiastes 3:11), and His Word. In His Word, we see God's greatest revelation of Himself in the incarnation of Christ for our salvation.

Want to know God better? He's waiting for you in His Word.

What can I do, right here,
right now, to know God better?

BETTER DAYS AHEAD

For we through the Spirit wait for the
hope of righteousness by faith.

GALATIANS 5:5

Few things are worse than feeling hopeless. When we feel like a difficult situation won't improve in our job, marriage, or any other important aspect of life, it can be overwhelming.

But thanks to Jesus' finished work on the cross, every Christian can experience life-changing hope through faith in Him. God-given faith produces "the hope of righteousness." This is hope that the righteousness of Christ is ours through faith; God has accepted His Son's payment for our sins; Jesus is returning one day to redeem His people; we will be made fully righteous, like Jesus, at His coming; all pain, suffering, sadness, hopelessness, and death will cease; and we will be with the Lord forever.

So take heart, friend. Faith in Christ produces a sure and glorious hope that better days are ahead—an eternity of righteousness with our great Redeemer.

What can I do, right here, right now,
to hope in righteousness by faith?

INCENSE OF THE SAINTS

Let my prayer be set forth before You as incense,
and the lifting up of my hands as the evening sacrifice.
PSALM 141:2

As God was giving Moses instructions for the tabernacle at Mount Sinai, He commanded Israel to make "an altar to burn incense on" (Exodus 30:1) with explicit instructions for its construction and use (verses 1–10) and for incense ingredients (verses 34–38). The priests were to burn incense morning and evening to God.

Why did God command this? Are there some dank, dingy corners of heaven that need a little freshening up? No, of course not.

This beautiful ritual was meant to symbolize our prayers (Luke 1:10; Revelation 5:8; 8:3–4). Just like modern-day aromatic candles and incense sticks fill our homes with pleasant fragrances, God delights in the prayers of His people that rise to heaven.

Our prayers are never a bother to God, nor should they be a drag to us. If we truly saw them for what they are in God's eyes, what might that do to our often-stale prayer lives?

What can I do, right here, right now,
to offer the sacrifice of holy prayer to God?

GUARDING THE GATE

Set a watch, O LORD, before my mouth;
watch over the door of my lips.

PSALM 141:3

In ancient times, guards were set on the walls and gates of a city. Their purpose was obvious: to protect the city against any destructive forces that wished to enter.

But in Psalm 141:3, King David flipped the metaphor. He asked God to help him guard his mouth. He wasn't concerned about what was *entering* his mouth. He didn't want any destructive forces to *leave* it.

Our mouths can do much good—and great harm. They can plant seeds of love, joy, and peace. But they can also destroy like a raging wildfire (James 3:5–6). They can bring much healing, and they can also inflict deadly poison (James 3:8).

As followers of Christ, we must tame our tongues and be disciplined with our speech. As Ephesians 4:29 says, let's use our mouth "for. . .edifying, that it may minister grace to the hearers."

What can I do, right here, right now, to guard my mouth and speak words of God's love?

UNSTOPPABLE PURPOSE

*"I know that You can do everything and that
no thought can be withheld from You."*

JOB 42:2

Job had just been through the worst life could offer. He had lost virtually his entire family and all his fortune. He had suffered an excruciating physical malady. He questioned God's goodness and purpose for these seemingly inexplicable trials.

Then God answered. He never explained His reasoning for Job's agonizing hardships. Instead, the Lord reminded Job who's God and who's not.

God had a great purpose for Job, but He didn't feel the need to fully explain Himself. In God's responses, it was as if He was telling Job, "Trust Me." In the end, Job acknowledged God's mysterious yet perfect sovereignty.

God has His purposes—sometimes mysterious, but always good—and they cannot be thwarted. When mystifying trials hit, remember the example of Job. God will accomplish all His purposes. Even though we might not understand, they are always good. In the midst of it, He says, "Trust Me."

**What can I do, right here, right now, to better
trust in God's unstoppable purposes?**

THE GREAT HOPE
OF THE CHURCH

*"Let us be glad and rejoice and give honor to
Him, for the marriage of the Lamb has come,
and His wife has made herself ready."*

REVELATION 19:7

✛

Hope is a powerful thing.

Hope pushes us forward. Hope keeps us on the right path. Hope helps us continue climbing when the way is rocky and steep. Hope provides joy throughout the journey.

As the church of the living God, our greatest hope is not in a new, state-of-the-art worship center or more adult Sunday school class space, or the talented new senior pastor coming on staff.

The great hope of the church is the second coming. Jesus, our Bridegroom, will return for His bride and bring us to the marriage celebration of the Lamb—worshipping in our Savior's presence as we enjoy the new heavens and new earth forever.

Life is hard and the future isn't always clear. But remember your true Hope. Jesus is coming back. The Cornerstone of the church will return to redeem His own.

**What can I do, right here, right now,
to hope and rejoice in Jesus' future return?**

OUT-OF-THIS-WORLD JOY

*You will show me the path of life.
In Your presence is fullness of joy; at Your right
hand there are pleasures forevermore.*

PSALM 16:11

God has graciously given us so much to be thankful for in this life. From daily material provisions of sustenance to the incredible spiritual realities of our salvation, we have much to rejoice in.

Yet these things are but a glimpse of what's to come. In a sin-stained world filled with pain, suffering, sadness, and death, the ultimate joy we seek is still on the horizon.

But it's coming.

Take heart, Christian. A day is approaching when we will experience "fullness of joy." It will be a far greater joy than we've ever experienced before. Joy that is perfect. Exciting. Fully satisfying. Incomparable. Unending.

Our mortal experience causes skepticism. *Can it really be?* Yes! It will come in immortality, in God's presence. There, at His right hand, we will enjoy "pleasures forevermore."

**What can I do, right here, right now,
to anticipate the coming fullness of
joy I'll experience in heaven?**

GLORIOUS FUTURE

*"God shall wipe away all tears from their eyes,
and there shall be no more death or sorrow or
crying, nor shall there be any more pain, for
the former things have passed away."*

REVELATION 21:4

✦

In a fallen world filled with much grief, it's hard to imagine an existence completely devoid of pain, suffering, and sadness. Yet when we read Revelation 21–22, we are presented with a future reality that seems too good to be true.

Standing in the presence of the triune God, we will be forever changed, and mortality will be a memory. Trials? Tribulations? Sin? Sadness? Sickness? Suffering? Death? All gone—never to return.

Our finite minds, limited by our humanity and flooded with worldly cares, wonder, *Will it really come true?* Yes, as certain as there's a God in heaven.

This is our sure hope, friend. Christ secured it for us through His great sacrifice, and He's returning to claim His own. This is our peace. Our joy. Our longing.

Amen. Come, Lord Jesus!

**What can I do, right here, right now,
to prepare for Christ's return?**

AUTHOR BIO

Joshua Cooley is a *New York Times* bestselling author who has written a variety of books and devotionals for all ages, including *The One Year Devotions with Jesus*, *Heroes of the Bible Devotional*, and *The One Year Sports Devotions for Kids*. He has also written two children's picture books, *I Can't Believe My Eyes!* and *Empty!* In 2018, he teamed with Super Bowl LII MVP Nick Foles to co-author the star quarterback's bestselling memoir, *Believe It: My Journey of Success, Failure, and Overcoming the Odds*. Joshua lives in Durham, North Carolina. You can visit his website at www.joshuacooleyauthor.com.

SCRIPTURE INDEX

MORE GREAT STUFF FOR GUYS

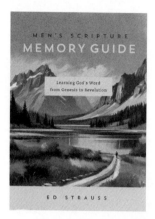

This powerful and practical guide is packed with invaluable information on scripture memorization. It lays out vital, need-to-know scriptures for your everyday life, plus much more—an overview of all 66 books of the Bible, helpful hints for retaining scripture, and a comprehensive list of Bible memory verses in biblical order.

Paperback / ISBN 979-8-89151-085-2